ENDORSEMENTS

"Do you ever feel that the darkness of this world is winning? Rebecca Nolley's study will give you the scriptural wisdom to *Shine* His light in this world. As a missionary in Uganda, and a true Bible student, Rebecca offers a richer perspective than many studies and equips you to bring the transforming power of the gospel to those who sit in darkness."

—Dee Brestin,
author of *Falling in Love with Jesus* and *Idol Lies*

"This timely and beautiful study has been deeply impactful for me. Packed full of truth, this study reminds us of our true mission—to be lights in this world as we reflect the light of our Savior. I would highly recommend this study to anyone looking for encouragement and refreshment. Rebecca's beautiful writing and wonderful teaching are sure to point you to the true Light of the World."

—Katie Davis Majors,
author of *Kisses from Katie* and *Daring to Hope*

"Rebecca Nolley's Bible study radiates God's great light. If you're looking for a study for your church, your community group, or even for personal use, the godly wisdom in *Shine* will ignite the participant's soul."

—Aubrey Sampson,
teaching pastor, contributor to Propel Women,
and author of *Overcomer* (Zondervan, 2015), *The Louder Song* (NavPress, 2020), and *Every Other Name* (NavPress, 2021)

"Great tool for discipleship!

I love Rebecca's heart for sharing the love of Christ with a hurting world! She makes you feel so comfortable as you travel through the Scriptures together, making meaningful stops along the way, learning how to share the light of Jesus Christ with others. You will be blessed as you glean wonderful truths about our Savior through this book. Well done!"

—Deb Weakly,
president of Help Club for Moms Ministries

BY

REBECCA NOLLEY

Shine: Being His Light in Darkness

Published by Deep River Books
Sisters, Oregon
www.deepriverbooks.com

ISBN – 13: 9781632695819
Library of Congress Control Number: 2021921626

Printed in the USA

Cover design by Robin Black, Inspirio Design

"Arise, shine for your light has come."

Isaiah 60:1

CONTENTS

Week 1:
Our Light Source

Day 1

THE BEGINNING

Ever since I was a little girl, I have loved the Christmas Eve service. There was always something magical about the candlelight service. As the congregation sang "Silent Night," the church lights would be turned off and darkness would envelop the room. Then suddenly the light of a single candle would penetrate the darkness. That light was used to light another candle, and one by one, the light of the candles was passed from person to person. The sanctuary slowly became aglow as lights were shared with neighbors until every person held a glowing candle in their hand. I remember a feeling of awe and peace, the challenge of trying to keep the wax from dripping off the paper, and the disappointment of having to blow out my candle when it was over. Though I didn't understand the significance of this tradition at the time, I knew it was beautiful and special, and that Christmas presents were soon to come.

Have you ever thought about why we have this tradition on Christmas Eve, a tradition that has been practiced since as far back as the Middle Ages in churches all over the world? Is it simply a "religious" tradition that inspires feelings of peace, awe, and joy? The significance of lighting candles on Christmas Eve is so much more than that. We light the candles to celebrate the One True Light. The One Light that came into this world and illuminated the darkness—Jesus. Not only did Jesus's light penetrate the darkness, but it continues to shine through you and me. And as it is shared, it grows brighter and brighter, just like those candles on Christmas

Eve. Lighting the candles is a sweet picture of the gospel and how the truth of the gospel penetrates the darkness and lights up the world.

That is what this Bible study is about—identifying the Light and becoming lights ourselves. We live in a dark world, and the darkness seems to be growing. Is that because we have hidden our light? Or have we failed to share it? Are our lights growing dimmer? Or maybe we just don't understand what being a light truly means. During the next eight weeks, we'll be going to God's Word to study the Giver of Light and how we can shine brighter for Him.

Let's begin this week by looking at the source of light. In order to understand the source, we need to start at the beginning—yes, the beginning of everything. Turn to the first verses of the Bible, which reveal the beginning of time.

Please read Genesis 1:1–5.

Look specifically at verses 1–2. What existed in the beginning?

Heavens & Earth, Ocean

Pause here for a few minutes. Even though these verses say "In the beginning," this wasn't the beginning of God. Look at Psalm 90:1–2. What do these verses say about our God?

He has been our dwelling place throughout all generations before the world was made.

What does God say about Himself in Revelation 1:8?

I am the Alpha & the Omega, who is, who was & who is to come, the Almighty.

God is eternal. He had no beginning and no end. 1 Timothy 1:17 says He is "the King of the ages, immortal." This truth can be hard for us time-constrained humans to fathom. We live in a world that revolves around time, but God does not. This "beginning" is the beginning of what we call time, the beginning of our universe and our existence.

Now look back at Genesis 1:3–5. What did God create first?

Light & separated it from darkness

How many times have you read this account of creation? If you are like me, you've heard or read it a dozen times. But there is something we can easily miss as we read or hear this account of the beginning of the world. Let me ask you to look closely at these verses. Where is the light coming from?

God

If your response was the sun, moon, and stars, look ahead to verses 14–19 in Genesis 1. On which day were those sources of light created?

4th Day

This is the astounding truth—God is our source of light. The world, the universe, needs no other light than that which He spoke into being. Theologian John Calvin said, "Therefore the Lord, by the very order of creation, bears witness that he holds in his hands the light, which he is able to impart to us without the sun and moon."[1] Now this can be a very complex idea, because when we say, "God is light" (1 John 1:5), this does not mean that God is the physical element of light. Yet light is the very essence of God, as seen in both His literal ability to shine and in the nonliteral way His light reveals truth, symbolizes all that is pure and good, and represents His glory. We'll continue to go deeper into this concept as this study continues.

The first verses in Genesis are not the only time we see God separating light and darkness. Another instance happened in the book of Exodus when the children of Israel were in bondage, and God sent plagues to reveal His power and to cause Pharaoh to release the Israelites. Turn to Exodus 10:21–23 and read these verses on the first plague. Can you explain where the darkness and light came from?

Moses stretched out his hand to the sky. Creating total darkness in Egypt except for the Isrealites.

As the "Father of lights" (James 1:17), God called light into being and controls the light and the darkness. God also created the objects that emanate light. Look again at Genesis 1:14–19 and list the reasons that God created these other light sources:

Create day & night. Mark sacred times, days & years.

These physical vessels of light are essential to our existence; however, there is a far more important purpose for the sun, moon, and stars. Record the following verses below:

Nehemiah 9:6

You alone are the Lord. You made the heavens, even the highest heavens & all their starry host, the earth & all that's on it, the seas & all that's in them. You give life to everything & the multitudes of heaven worship you.

Psalm 19:1–3

The heavens declare the glory of God, the skies proclaim the work of his hands. Day after day they pour forth speech, night after night they reveal knowledge. They have no speech, they use no words, no sound is heard from them.

Isaiah 40:26

Lift up your eyes & look to the heavens: Who created all these? He who brings out the starry host one by one & calls forth each of them by name. Because of his great power & mighty strength not one of them is missing.

According to these verses, what is the purpose of the heavenly lights?

Since creation, the brilliant sun, moon, and stars and the millions of galaxies have existed to declare God's glory to the world. "His eternal power and divine nature" (Romans 1:20) are clearly seen as we look up at the sky. He has magnificently made Himself known through the brilliance of the heavenly lights. How truly amazing our God is!

After looking at the creation of light today, let's end with praising the Creator and the Giver of all lights. The following is a benediction that Jews in Jesus's time likely recited before the Shema (the Jewish prayer spoken twice a day). As you read this prayer, use it to give God the praise and the glory He so richly deserves.

> Blessed be Thou, O Lord, King of the world, Who formest the light and createst the darkness, Who makest peace and createst everything; Who in mercy, givest light to the earth and to those who dwell upon it, and in Thy goodness day by day and every day renewest the works of creation. Blessed be the Lord our God for the glory of His handiwork and for the light-giving lights, which He has made for His praise, Selah! Blessed be the Lord our God, Who hath formed the lights.[2]

Day 2

THE END

Yesterday, we looked at the beginning. Today, we'll look at the end. But before we turn to the last book of the Bible, Revelation, go to the book of Isaiah in the Old Testament. The book of Isaiah references the end times of Revelation even though it was written between 740 and 681 BC. Read Isaiah 60:19–20 (ESV) to see what Isaiah prophesies about the end days and fill in the blanks below:

> The sun shall be no more
> your light by day,
> nor for brightness shall the moon
> give you light;
> but the Lord_______ will be your everlasting light,
> and your God will be your glory.
> Your sun shall no more go down,
> nor your moon withdraw itself;
> for the Lord_______ will be your everlasting light,
> and your days of mourning shall be ended.

According to these verses, where will our light come from in the end days?

The Lord

Now turn to Revelation and write down the following verses:

Revelation 21:23

The city does not need the sun or moon to shine on it, for the glory of God gives it light & the Lamb is it's lamp.

Revelation 22:5

There will be no more night. They will not need the light of a lamp or the light of the sun, for the Lord God will give them light. And they will reign forever & ever

Wow, it comes full circle! Like bookends the glory of the Lord provides all the light necessary both at the beginning of the world and at the end. The sun, moon, and stars are no longer required because His glory eradicates the darkness and shines forevermore. He is our Everlasting Light! Isn't that incredible? It thrills my soul to think of how glorious that day will be when we will walk in His light.

Now, let's go back and read these Scriptures in a bit more detail. Read Revelation 21:22–27, and then answer the following questions:

Who is the Lamb mentioned in verses 22–23? (Hint: Look up John 1:29)

Jesus

Though Jesus and God are one, they both shine in heaven and illuminate the City of God. Jesus, the Lamb of God, is the Light of the World both now and for all of eternity. We will discuss this more specifically over the next two days; however, this truth will resonate throughout the entire study.

According to verse 27, who shall walk in the light?

Only those who's names are written in the Lamb's book of life.

Take the opportunity to notice a few things from these verses. First, it says, "the nations of those who are saved" will walk in the light. Redeemed people from every tribe and every nation will be in heaven. Revelation 7:9 describes "a great multitude that no one could number, from every nation, from all tribes and peoples and languages, standing before the throne and before the Lamb." Does that bring you joy? Imagine all the different races, nationalities, and peoples gathering together, unified in their worship of God. This is what those who are saved have to look forward to.

Also notice that the gates will not be shut because there is no night. However, who or what will not be allowed in?

Nothing impure, shameful or deceitful.

This is both a sad and uplifting truth. It is uplifting in that no evil, no sin, no lies, nothing or no one that doesn't glorify God is allowed into heaven. Heaven will not be like this broken and sinful world. Hallelujah! However, it's also a great tragedy to think of all those who will not have access to heaven. We will discuss this further next week, but for now, spend a few minutes looking into what the Book of Life is. Look up a few of the following verses, and then answer the question on the next page.

Psalm 69:28

Malachi 3:16–18

Revelation 3:5

Revelation 20:12–15

After reading these passages, what does the Lamb's Book of Life mean to you?

Passage to heaven

As we conclude this lesson today, my prayer is that you know that your name is written in the Lamb's Book of Life, that you would be among the throngs of nations glorifying God the Father in heaven. May you look forward to experiencing, for yourself, God's glory illuminating the heavens, without need of the sun, moon, and stars. What a glorious future we have awaiting us!

Day 3

AND EVERYTHING IN-BETWEEN

We've looked at the beginning and the end, the first book of the Bible and the last. The Bible starts and ends with the light of God, yet we stand in the middle where the light of God isn't so easily seen. You see, not long after creation, sin entered the world and brought darkness, sin, and death. Go ahead and read all of Genesis 3 as a reminder of how sin entered the world. Then specifically record verse 15 below:

And I will put enmity between you & the woman & between your offspring & hers, he will crush your head, and you will strike his heel.

Even with the heavy consequence of sin, God gave a "Seed" of hope. This is the first prophecy of Jesus Christ! Whether your Bible uses the word "seed" or "offspring," it describes Jesus Christ, who will bruise the head of Satan. God, in His mercy and lovingkindness, did not leave us in our sin and darkness. He promised to send a light, and He fulfilled that promise in Jesus. Jesus is the hope of our salvation, the light that will permeate the darkness. Let's celebrate the light of Jesus over the next two days!

Though the name of Jesus doesn't come into the Scriptures until the New Testament, He is actually mentioned all throughout the Old

Testament. Time and time again, God reveals the promise of the Savior, Jesus Christ. In fact, there are over three hundred references to Christ in the Old Testament (though the exact number varies depending on the specifications). Take a look at three of these Scriptures:

First, read Numbers 24:17, which was written 1,400 years before Christ's birth.

How does a star represent Jesus Christ?

____

____

A scepter is a staff representing authority. How does this symbolize Jesus?

____

____

Next, look at Isaiah 9:1–7, written 700 years before Jesus came to earth.

In verse 2, who is the great light the people who walk in darkness will see? What other names are given to Him?

____

____

Now read Malachi 4:2, which was written about 400 years before Jesus was born.

How is Jesus described here?

____

____

Notice the aspects of light that depict our Savior, Jesus. We'll continue to see this connection between light and Jesus as we turn to the New Testament. The New Testament is the fulfillment of the hope and expectations presented in the Old Testament. As we turn to the New Testament, let's first look at what Zechariah prophesied about Jesus before He was born. Zechariah, a priest and the father of John the Baptist, eagerly anticipated the coming of the Savior and made this prophesy when his son was born.

Read Luke 1:76–79.

How does verse 78 describe Jesus?

____

____

What will He accomplish as stated in verse 79?

____

____

I just love how these verses describe Jesus, don't you? Some versions say, "the sunrise shall visit us," and others say, "the dayspring from on high," both of which are beautiful representations of Jesus's coming. Think of the last sunrise you saw—the brilliant rays of red and gold, calling the day into being and taking away the darkness of night. Isn't that what Jesus does in our lives? He shines into the darkness and awakens us with His glory and beauty.

You can also read this truth about Jesus in the book of John. John 1:1–12 (NKJV) is written below and continues on the next page. Underline the word "light" every time you see it.

> In the beginning was the Word, and the Word was with God, and the Word was God. He was in the beginning with God. All things were made through Him, and without Him nothing was made that was made. In Him was life, and the life was the light of men. And the light shines in the darkness, and the darkness did not comprehend it. There was a man sent from God, whose name was John. This man came for a witness, to bear witness of the Light, that all through him might believe. He was not that

> Light, but was sent to bear witness of that Light. That was the true Light which gives light to every man coming into the world. He was in the world, and the world was made through Him, and the world did not know Him. He came to His own, and His own did not receive Him. But as many as received Him, to them He gave the right to become children of God, to those who believe in His name.

John describes Jesus in such a beautiful way. Name three ways John describes Jesus:

____

____

Notice when the word "light" is capitalized. What does this signify?

____

____

What do you think it means that "the darkness did not comprehend the light"?

____

____

Not only did Zechariah and John present Jesus as our Light, but Jesus speaks this truth about Himself. Write down what He says in John 8:12:

____

____

____

Now the timing of Jesus declaring Himself as light is extremely significant. The Feast of Tabernacles had taken place that week, beginning with a ceremony called the Illumination of the Temple. During this nighttime ceremony, four massive candelabra would be lit in the temple treasury. These candelabra were described to be as tall as the temple wall, which created flames that illuminated all of the temple and surrounding Jerusalem. It was after this ceremony in the temple treasury, with the extinguished flames of the torches behind Him, that Jesus declared Himself the Light of the World.[3] He is the light, and the beautiful truth is that His light will never be extinguished.

God, as the source of light, gave us Jesus as the One True Light that will illuminate the darkness of this world and bring us hope and salvation. I feel like this is something that we can easily take for granted. Jesus is our light! What does that mean to you personally? Please give a personal response on what it means to you that Jesus is your light, and tomorrow we'll discuss Jesus further.

Day 4

JESUS'S TRIUMPH OVER DARKNESS

Do you remember on day 2 when we looked at the Lamb's Book of Life in the book of Revelation? If you weren't sure whether your name is in the Lamb's Book of Life, this lesson is for you. In fact, it's for all of us, because Jesus is where our life and our salvation are found. We were all lost in darkness—in sin and death—but Jesus came into that darkness and shone a great light into our hearts. He is our Savior and our Light!

Dear sister, here is the truth: Light overcomes the darkness and will someday destroy it for all of eternity. It is as the Lady says in C. S. Lewis's *The Great Divorce*: "Here is the joy that cannot be shaken. Our light can swallow up your darkness; but your darkness cannot now infect our light."[4] You see, the battle was won on the cross. In that dark hour on the cross, death was defeated, our sin forgiven, and the battle won! "It is finished!" (John 19:30) The words of Jesus not only signified His death, but life!

Right before Jesus was crucified on the cross, He said to his disciples, "I will no longer talk much with you, for the ruler of this world is coming. He has no claim on me, but I do as the Father has commanded me, so that the world may know that I love the Father" (John 14:30–31).

Jesus himself said, "He has __________ claim over me!" Yet He submitted himself to God's will. Why did Jesus do what the Father asked?

Obedience and love are intertwined. This point will be further addressed in the course of this study, but for now, think about how this could relate to you. What are your reasons for obeying God? Do they echo why Jesus obeyed Him?

Read what Jesus calls the hour in Luke 22:52–53. What does Jesus say about this hour?

We'll see this truth fulfilled as we turn to the next chapter of Luke and read about Jesus's death. Please take your time in reading Luke 23:24–47 and contemplate the magnitude of Christ's death. Then answer the following question:

What happened between the sixth and ninth hours (verses 44–45)?

Now the sixth and ninth hours are from 12 (noon) to 3 p.m., so in the middle of the day. The ESV describes the sun's light as failing, and other versions say, "the sun was darkened," which some tend to believe describes an eclipse. But even if it had been an eclipse, it would have been miraculous, as a three-hour eclipse when the moon is full is a scientific impossibility.[5] We know the moon was full the previous night, because the Passover always falls on a full moon. Though we may not be able to understand how the sun could go dark, we see that this was God's doing. This darkness not only signified death and sorrow but was also a sign of God's judgment. You can read similar descriptions in Scriptures such as Joel 2:1–2, Zephaniah 1:14–15, and Acts 2:20. In fact, look at the similarities between this moment and what Amos describes in Amos 8:9–10, written below:

> "And on that day," declares the Lord God,
> "I will make the sun go down at noon
> and darken the earth in broad daylight.
> I will turn your feasts into mourning
> and all your songs into lamentation;
> I will bring sackcloth on every waist
> and baldness on every head;
> I will make it like the mourning for an only son
> and the end of it like a bitter day."

It's okay if God's judgment scares you. It should! He will judge the world for its sin and evil. However, even in this dark moment of judgment, we see the beauty of redemption. First, among the two criminals that were executed with Jesus, one of them recognized Him as Lord, and Jesus forgave him at that very moment (Luke 23:39–43). Isn't that an incredible picture of the grace of God? Within minutes before taking his last breath, the criminal didn't have to do anything other than believe that Jesus was Lord, and he was saved.

We also see that the temple curtain, which separated the Holiness of God from men, was torn (verse 45). You see, in the Old Testament, God's presence resided in His temple within the inner curtain. No one, except for the high priest, had access, and that was only after a sacrifice was made. Yet through Christ's sacrifice, we now have access to God. His death made atonement for our sin, and we now "have confidence to enter the holy places by the blood of Jesus, by the new and living way that he opened for us through the curtain, that is, through the flesh" (Hebrews 10:19–20).

And what should our response be to this incredible sacrifice? I hope it is the same as the centurion in verse 47. What did he do?

Though it was given reign for a moment, the power of darkness was defeated on the cross. To those who believe, "He has delivered us from the domain of darkness and transferred us to the kingdom of his beloved Son, in whom we have redemption, the forgiveness of sins" (Colossians 1:13–14). He has delivered us from darkness. There is still a battle going on, but the final victory has been won!

And now you have a choice. Do you receive this salvation and become a child of God like that criminal on the cross, or do you continue to live in darkness and sin? God has delivered us from the power of darkness, but He doesn't force us to believe that Jesus died to take the punishment of our sins. If you've never accepted this truth but would like to, all you have to do is put your faith in Jesus. Confess your disbelief and sin, repent, and turn your life over to Him. Believe who God says He is: your Creator, your Redeemer, and your Light. Take the next moment to pray to receive His salvation, and if you already have, take the time to thank God for His deliverance from darkness.

Praise God! Dear sister, you are a child of God! Whether you prayed for the first time or did so many years ago, you are walking in His light. Let's end today reflecting on the magnitude of what Christ has done for you. Sit at His feet and worship Him, thanking Him for all he has done.

Day 5

OUR HELPER AND THE WORD

The summer after I graduated college, I accepted a teaching job in Colorado Springs. That July, we put my meager belongings in a small U-Haul, and my parents drove me from Illinois to Colorado. I'll never forget the feeling when they said goodbye, turned the U-Haul around, and left me. Looking out the window of that teeny tiny apartment in a town in which I knew nobody, I'd never felt so alone.

I'm so grateful that Jesus did not leave us that way. When Jesus left this earth over two thousand years ago, He did not just drop us off, return to His heavenly home, and say, "good luck." He did not leave us alone. Read what Jesus said in John 14:26.

Who did Jesus leave, and what was His role?

....

....

For all who believe, Jesus left a helper, one who would "dwell in you" (1 Corinthians 3:16). We can't neglect the Holy Spirit as a source of light. Though no direct Scripture depicts the Holy Spirit as light, Scripture does depict that God, Jesus, and the Holy Spirit are One. From the very beginning they've existed together. "Let *us* make man in our image" (Genesis 1:26).

Look up the following verses. Copy them below and circle the references to God, put a square around the references to Jesus, and underline the references to the Holy Spirit.

Matthew 28:19

John 15:26

God the Father, Jesus the Son, and the Holy Spirit are three entities in One Supreme Being. This coexistence is also known as the Trinity. And since God and Jesus are our light, so is the Holy Spirit. The Holy Spirit is also referred to as the Spirit of wisdom (Ephesians 1:17–18), which will "enlighten our hearts." Often, in Scripture, wisdom is associated with light or that which illuminates truth. The Spirit imparts "light" into our lives.

Read John 16:13–14 below, and underline what the Spirit will do for us:

> When the Spirit of truth comes, he will guide you into all the truth, for he will not speak on his own authority, but whatever he hears he will speak, and he will declare to you the things that are to come. He will glorify me, for he will take what is mine and declare it to you.

See, unlike the time I was left in Colorado Springs to find my way and figure it out on my own, Jesus left someone to guide us. With the Spirit as our light, we can transverse this earth knowing God's will for our lives.

Not only did Jesus leave the Holy Spirit as a light to guide us and give us wisdom, but He also recognized our need for something tangible.

The Bible that you and I are reading for this study is a physical, concrete instrument left for us.

Write down Psalm 119:105.

____

____

What does this mean to you? In your own words, describe how His Word acts as a light.

____

____

____

Picture yourself on a hike in the woods. Your hike takes longer than you had planned, and it becomes dark. It's a cloudy night, so the moon and stars can't light your way. You don't know which way to turn, if you should go forward or backward, and you can't see the obstacles in front of you. What is needed and necessary to direct you? A flashlight or a lamp to light your way. That is what the Word of God is to us. It is the lamp to guide our feet and a light that illuminates the path ahead of us. The Word of God helps us to know which way to turn, when to stop, and when to move forward. Without it, we would just stumble through life, not knowing what direction to go. As Psalm 119:130 says, "The unfolding of your words gives light; it imparts understanding to the simple." The Bible guides us, illuminates the truth of who God is, and reveals our sin and need for a Savior.

Wouldn't it be a shame to have access to a light but never use it? To continue to stumble through the darkness even though the flashlight is in your pocket? This is the reality in which most people live. The light is there, but unused. Can I ask you a personal question? How often are you in the Word of God? Ponder this question as we continue. God's Word is meant to be used every day, for every circumstance, and for every need. I think for many of us, we are just too busy or don't even recognize God's

Word as our light, so we do the best we can on our own, stumbling along in darkness.

In order to use your Bible as a light, first you have to believe in the Bible. Do you believe that the Bible is true? We'll come back to that question. First, let's look at 2 Timothy 3:16–17. Write down these verses below.

The English Standard Version says "breathed," and in other versions, this verse says "inspired." Look up the word "inspired." In your own words, what does it mean that all Scripture is inspired by God?

God's written Word, the Bible, is His breath, breathed into the ears of man and given shape into written words. I understand that it is difficult for people to believe the entirety of the Bible. How can we take a book written by approximately forty authors over a course of 1500 years and trust it? It's actually the *why* that we can trust it that brings us to the *how*. Why can we trust God's Word? We can trust the Word of God because He created us, He loves us, and He does not lie. Hebrews 6:18 says, "It is impossible for God to lie." Once we are rooted in the truth of His unfailing love for us, then it is through faith that we believe that He purposed every book, every chapter, every word for His glory and for our good. So let's return to the question: Do you believe in the entirety of the Bible? If you don't, what parts, or what aspects, are hard for you to believe?

It's okay to be honest with yourself. There are many people who only believe in certain parts of the Bible, such as certain books, or even take out certain verses. But if this is you, I encourage you to pursue the truth. Because, as we'll discuss next week, using only parts of the Bible (the parts that we like, the parts that work for us) is a method that Satan uses to pull us away from the truth.

Please pray through this, talk to someone about your doubts, seek godly counsel, and look to His Word. Do your own research instead of taking my word or someone else's word for it. Don't allow your doubts to get in the way of truly knowing God's Word. I pray that as you seek out the truth and complete this Bible study, you will see the authority and light of His Word—His entire Word.

Now, go back to 2 Timothy 3:16–17. What does it say about the profit of Scripture?

As we spend time in God's Word, we are equipped to face this world and do the work that God has for us. Just as light equips us to see and do the tasks before us, God's Word equips us for this life and for the work God has for us. And as God's Word dwells in you, so does His light, because His Word is light. We'll definitely need the light of His Word throughout this study to illuminate God's truth to us, to shine in us and through us.

So, let's review this week. What are our sources of light? God as the Creator of light, Jesus as the Light of the World, the Bible as the light of His Word, and the Holy Spirit that enlightens truth will all illuminate this dark world we live in. Rejoice in this gift, dear sister—that we have His light to guide us, to instruct us, and to give us hope. May His light shine upon you today as you dwell on the Scriptures we had for this week.

Week 2: The Darkness

Day 1

WHAT IS THE DARKNESS?

In order to understand the light, we need to spend some time identifying the darkness. I'm cautious about spending too much time studying darkness. Too many people worship the darkness instead of the light. Too many people are drawn to the darkness instead of the light. I want us to know what we are up against, but without getting caught up in trying to understand the ways of the darkness. Instead, let us focus on the goodness of the light and the power it has over darkness.

Before we study darkness this week, write down what darkness means to you:

____

____

In Scripture, darkness is either seen literally, as the absence of light, or figuratively, referring to something that is secret, or to that which is sinful or evil. Scripture is full of references to darkness in opposition to light. We'll be looking at quite a few today so that we can better understand what darkness implies.

First, turn to the book of Proverbs, which has many references to light and darkness. Read Proverbs 4:18–19 and compare the two paths below:

The Path of the Righteous	The Path of the Wicked

Earlier Proverbs talks about those "who forsake the paths of uprightness to walk in the ways of darkness" (Proverbs 2:13). Let me ask you: Do you see a middle road here? That's because there isn't one. Scripture clearly depicts the choice between the two paths we can take, the path of righteousness and the path of darkness, with no in-between. The struggle is that the path of wickedness, or sin, is easy, and the path of righteous living is difficult. As Matthew 7:13–14 says, "Enter by the narrow gate. For the gate is wide and the way is easy that leads to destruction, and those who enter by it are many. For the gate is narrow and the way is hard that leads to life, and those who find it are few."

What do you think are some reasons that the way leading to destruction is easy but that which leads to life is hard?

Unfortunately, we live in a world that loves sin and hates the light. In John 3:19, Jesus said, "The light has come into the world, and people loved the darkness rather than the light, because their works were evil."

Take a look at a few of these evil works as described in Job 24:13–16.

What characterizes those who rebel against the light?

____

____

In what ways is darkness a tool for those who do evil?

____

____

Again, I want you to recognize the extreme separation between light and darkness because that is how God views it. Light is the complete opposite of darkness. There is not this blending that we often see around us. Take the time to look at one more Scripture to further prove this point. Write down 2 Corinthians 6:14–15 below:

____

____

____

____

____

You may have heard this verse used in reference to marriage, warning a believer not to marry a nonbeliever. However, this warning is not only for the context of marriage, but for every aspect of life. Verse 15 is a command to stop your partnership with unbelievers and the evil works in the world around you. It then goes on to ask four questions, showing that these extremes cannot coexist. You cannot join together light and darkness. In the same way, it is impossible for Christ and Belial (another name for Satan) to live in harmony together.

Now, there is a difference between having partnership with (being yoked to) those who are walking in darkness and lawlessness and purposefully being a light and sharing God's love with those who are in darkness. What do you think that difference is?

Sometimes we play dangerously close to the boundaries of sin for the sake of "being relevant." We don't want to draw that line in the sand, so we try to exist in the gray, desiring to be perceived as tolerant. I hope you see from these verses that it's not possible to choose a middle road. Compromise will not penetrate the darkness. The light of the gospel will penetrate the darkness. We need to connect to unbelievers in a way that does not compromise the gospel and what the Bible says.

Think about what this means to you personally. Do you have some "mixing" that is in your life that you need to separate from?

This is a question that I continually ask myself: How do I live in this dark world and reach those who live in darkness without compromising the truth of the gospel? It isn't easy, and we'll continue to look at how to do this throughout this study. For now, I want you to go back to the first question on what darkness means to you. After reading these Scriptures, what is the Lord revealing to you? Is your definition of darkness different? Record your thoughts below.

Day 2

THE PRINCE OF DARKNESS

It is with good reason that Martin Luther labeled Satan as "the Prince of Darkness" in his hymn "A Mighty Fortress Is Our God." He is the Prince of Darkness, and he has come to "kill and destroy" (John 10:10). Let's look at 2 Corinthians 4:3–4 to see how he might accomplish this.

Whom does "the god of this world" refer to?

....

....

What does the god of this world do and why?

....

....

Darkness blinds us. In the physical sense, we cannot see what is around us when it is dark. In the spiritual sense, the darkness blinds us to the truth of who God is, to what He has done for us, and to our sin. This Scripture describes a veil covering the minds and hearts of those who are perishing in order to blind them. That is not to say that the gospel itself is veiled. It is their minds (and hearts) that are kept from seeing the truth. Calvin stated it like this: "the blindness of unbelievers in no way detracts from the clearness of the gospel, for the sun is not less resplendent because the blind do not perceive it."[6]

Satan, the Devil, Beelzebub, and Lucifer are all names of the evil one who is referred to as the ruler of this world in multiple passages of Scripture, including 1 John 5:19. Record that verse below:

But how can the whole world be in the power of the evil one? Isn't God the ruler of this world? Remember, we've discussed how the battle was already won on the cross and how in John 14:30, Jesus said, "The ruler of this world is coming. He has no claim on me." Even though Satan has been given (a key word) temporary rule over this world, he is not the ultimate ruler. His reign will end, and he will be destroyed. Have you ever wondered how Satan came to be a part of this world? There are two specific Scriptures that give us clues to what happened. Look them up below, and then record what they say about what happened to Satan.

Isaiah 14:12–15

Ezekiel 28:12–19

From these Scriptures, what led to Satan's downfall and being cast out of heaven?

Keep this in mind as we continue, because you'll find that Satan will tempt us to fall the same way he did.

Now look at Ephesians 4:17–18.

What characterizes "the Gentiles" in this passage?

What/who do you think causes this blindness/darkness (or hardness of hearts)?

Psalm 36:1–2 says, "Transgression speaks to the wicked deep in his heart; there is no fear of God before his eyes. For he flatters himself in his own eyes that his iniquity cannot be found out and hated." You see, a prideful person cannot even see his or her own sin or iniquity. Pride darkens our understanding and leads us into a state of blindness. The *Oxford Dictionary of English* defines pride as "a feeling of deep pleasure or satisfaction derived from one's own achievements."[7] In other words, pride is feeling that we can do it all on our own, that we don't need God, and that our self-worth is in "our" achievements. C. S. Lewis says, "Pride leads to every other vice: it is the complete anti-God state of mind."[8] Why would pride be the anti-God state of mind? Because God created us to rely on Him! Our self-worth can only be found in Him and His achieving work on the cross.

What do you do when you are blind? You fall! As Proverbs 16:18 says, "Pride goes before destruction, and a haughty spirit before a fall." This is exactly what led Satan to his fall and destruction, and it continues to lead to our fall and destruction. The thing about being blind is that you don't always know what you should be seeing. We were all born into a state of blindness (Psalm 51:5), and we often don't recognize the sin that is in our lives.

So let's take some time today and look at our own lives. Do you have pride that is causing blindness to the sin that is in your life? Is there anything you need to confess or repent from?

Even though darkness causes blindness, light causes sight! Remember, God has called you out of darkness and into His light. We don't need to fear the darkness, but instead, be aware of the damage and harm that it can do in our lives and in the lives of others.

Day 3

HOW SATAN BLINDS US

Yesterday, we discussed how Satan rules this world with the intent to blind us. Today, we'll discuss two of the methods Satan uses to blind us. The first is to use lies and manipulating Scripture, and the second is to use hate. Let's begin with looking at how Satan uses lies and the manipulation of Scripture to draw us away from the light.

Write down John 8:44:

Who is saying this, and what does the "beginning" refer to?

Go ahead and read Genesis 2:16–17 to look at the beginning. What instructions did God give to Adam in the garden?

Now, compare those instructions to what Satan says to Eve in Genesis 3:1–5. What are the differences?

Satan truly is the "father of lies," as seen from this first moment that he steps into the picture. This is the complete opposite of God. Remember, it is impossible for God to lie. Numbers 23:19 says, "God is not a man, that he should lie." In contrast, lying is one of Satan's favorite strategies. He loves to take truth, warp it, and make it "sound" like truth. However, his manipulation takes God's truth, holiness, and sovereignty out of the picture.

We can clearly see how the devil used this tactic when Jesus was taken into the wilderness to be tempted. Read Matthew 4:1–11 and compare what the devil said with the truth of the Scripture. Take a look at each of the temptations, as well as the Scripture that Jesus used in defense. Then write down the lie and the truth using the chart below.

Temptation (Lie)	Truth (Scripture Jesus Used)
1.	(Deuteronomy 8:3)
2.	(Deuteronomy 6:16)
3.	(Deuteronomy 6:13)

Jesus demonstrated how we are to know the Word of God in order to defeat temptation. So many times, we are persuaded by false truths because we don't have a full knowledge and understanding of the Word of God. Remember, if the Word of God is our light, we need to use it to illuminate these half-truths. We must have the knowledge base to know when people are using Scripture out of context or manipulating it for their own ambition.

What is frightening is that the devil also knows the Word of God! In the second temptation, the devil referenced Psalm 91:11–12, yet he took it out of context and manipulated it to his own means.

The last verses of the Bible warn us against these manipulations. Read Revelation 22:18–19. What does this Scripture say?

The fact is that there are many world religions that use the Bible. However, any Scripture that is taken out of context, thrown in with other "prophet's" words, or used without regard for the entirety of the Bible is deceiving people. Can I stop you for a moment to ask you to pray? Thinking about how many people are blinded and how Satan actually uses Scripture as a tool to lead people away from their Creator fills me with sadness. First, let's pray for our own hearts to stay true to God's Word and His truth; that we would stand strong in not allowing our hearts and minds to be misguided. Then, pray for all those who are walking around this world blind, stumbling in the darkness. Pray that they would see the truth and light of His Word. If you want to list specific people or write out your prayer, you can do so below.

Another method Satan uses in order to blind us is hate. Hate puts blinders over our eyes, and we lose perspective. We cannot see our own pride, selfishness, and sin. Read 1 John 2:9–11.

How do these verses describe those who hate their brother?

How do you think it's possible to believe you are in the light but actually be in the darkness?

Who do you think "brother" is referring to in this Scripture?

John is writing to his fellow brethren in the church, so when he says "brother," he is actually referring to those who are in Christ—our Christian brothers and sisters. We must start by loving those who are in the body of Christ. However, don't deceive yourself into saying that you only must love those who are in Christ. The Bible is clear in that we are to love ALL people. Jesus says, "Love your enemies, and pray for those who persecute you" (Matthew 5:44). Beyond our fellow brothers and sisters in Christ, we are to love all of mankind, even our enemies. Why? Because every person is made in the image of God! Later in Matthew 5, Jesus says, "For if you love those who love you, what reward do you have? Do not even the tax collectors do the same? And if you greet only your brothers, what more are you doing than others? Do not even the Gentiles do the same? You therefore must be perfect, as your heavenly Father is perfect" (Matthew 5:46–48). Unfortunately, there is a lot of hate going on right now. You hear it in the news, see it on Facebook, and read it in blog posts. The sad reality is that a lot of "Christians" are doing the hating.

There was an instance several years back, the year we were moving to Uganda, in which my husband, Kent, was accosted. He had been preaching at church on a Sunday morning, and it was between services. He had forgotten something in the car, so he quickly walked out to the parking lot, grabbed the item, and then returned to preach. Later that evening, he received an extremely heated email. The person writing the email had been in the parking lot when Kent had gone out and evidently had spoken a greeting. This individual was outraged that my "missionary/pastor" husband would think so highly of himself that he wouldn't even greet people from the congregation. Of course, Kent had no idea that he had done this. He hadn't seen or heard this individual, as he was extremely overwhelmed and not paying attention when he quickly walked out to his car. Though his accusations were untrue, his email was very hurtful. It caused me to think, How often do I make the same mistake? I assume the worst—that the person must not like me, that the action was done intentionally—and quickly pass judgment. Instead, I have the opportunity to give the benefit of the doubt. What if instead of becoming belligerent at my husband, that individual had sent an email asking Kent if he was okay? Responding in love, giving grace, and assuming the best will help us avoid jumping to hateful conclusions.

Write about a time you may have had someone assume the worst about you like this or a time you may have done it yourself:

____

____

____

I love the following quote from Dr. Martin Luther King Jr. Read it and write what it means to you below: "Darkness cannot drive out darkness, only light can do that. Hate cannot drive out hate, only love can do that."

____

____

____

Look a little further in 1 John, and record 1 John 4:20–21 below:

____

____

____

This is a powerful verse! We can't love God and hate our brother at the same time! Why do you think that is?

As we love our brother, "we abide in the light and there is no cause for stumbling." I love that we don't stumble because we have the light. We can see where to go and what we need to do. We'll talk more about this over the course of this study, but I just want us to take a few minutes to look at our own lives. Is there any hatred in your heart that is causing you to be in the darkness? Remember, sometimes we can't even see our own hatred because we are blinded, so you may need to ask those closest to you. Hatred can come in the form of unforgiveness, biases, judgment, resentment, and/or anger toward a particular person or a people group. If so, confess it and pray for love. It may take a while, and it may not be easy, but I pray we can all recognize any hate that is in our hearts and the blindness that it causes.

Day 4

THE DARKNESS OF HELL IS REAL

This is probably the hardest lesson for me to write. I can't do it without weeping. The reality of hell is so heavy, so horrible, and so real that it puts a weight on my soul that I cannot lift. Yet I cannot talk about darkness without clarifying what is considered the "outer darkness" or the "blackness of darkness forever." Those are two of the many descriptions of hell from Scripture.

There are those who say hell isn't real. I'm not going to debate that, and I pray that by just reading the Bible and what it says about hell, you will come to realize that it is very much real. God doesn't lie. The devil does. He would love for you to think hell isn't real so that you don't have to worry about your salvation or the salvation of others. I by no means want to dictate your belief but want you to look at God's Word for what it says.

Hell is not a topic to be taken lightly. I mean, it's people's eternities we are talking about! I take the topic of today very seriously and with great thought and prayer. I would never want to lead people astray. So, let's look at the Scriptures today with fear and trembling, asking the Lord to reveal His truth to us. My prayer is that the Sprit would teach you according to His Word.

Hell is described in many ways, but one resounding way is using the term darkness. Please look up these Scriptures in the ESV and fill in the blanks.

1 Samuel 2:9 "He will guard the feet of his faithful ones, but the wicked shall be cut off in ________________________."

Matthew 8:12 "The sons of the kingdom will be thrown into the ____ ____. In that place there will be weeping and gnashing of teeth."

2 Peter 2:4 "For if God did not spare the angels when they sinned, but cast them into hell and committed them to chains of _______________ ___________________ to be kept until the judgment . . ."

I want you to consider this truth: In Him there is no darkness. Darkness cannot exist with God. Write 1 John 1:5 below:

....

....

....

You see, darkness cannot be in the presence of God. Those who continue to walk in darkness and choose to follow the "god of this world" will be separated from God. That is what the truth of hell is. It is complete separation from God, which also means separation from all that is good, holy, pure, and righteous. Can you imagine taking all the good, all the love, and all that is righteous out of this earth and leaving the ugliness, the evil, and the sin? That is just a glimpse of what hell is like.

Read 2 Thessalonians 1:3–10 and answer the questions below:

According to verse 8, who will be punished?

....

....

How will they be punished (verse 9)?

....

....

The absence of God's power and glory is the full extent of hell. I can't begin to describe the rest of it or understand it in my own frail humanness. All I know is that I don't want to be separated from God's holiness, His love, or His presence, and I don't want others to be separated either! This reality should stir our hearts to be a light in this dark world and to pray for those who are facing eternal darkness.

Though there are many other Scriptures we could look at, I want us to consider one more for today. Read the parable in Matthew 13:24–30 and then its explanation in verses 36–43.

Who are the "weeds," and what will happen to them during the harvest?

Who are the "good seeds," and what will happen to them during the harvest time?

What does this verse mean to you? "Then the righteous will shine like the sun in the kingdom of their Father. He who has ears, let him hear" (verse 43).

These are difficult verses to read, and they may stir in you fear, frustration, or even resentment. Let me encourage you, dear sister, that even within these verses of coming judgment, we can see God's love. Look back at verse 29. Why does God not want the weeds taken out before the right time?

God is just! I'm reminded of how many times in Scripture we see God preserving the righteous among the wicked. The story of Noah

(Genesis 6:5–18) and the story of Lot (Genesis 18:20–19:29) are a couple of examples of God saving the few righteous people before destroying the wicked. We have this assurance that God will do what is right and just. He will preserve and keep those who are righteous and who serve God.

Consider in your heart what the Bible says about hell. It's something that we don't like to think about, so we don't. But I'm asking you to think about it. Seek out what you believe about hell, look into other Scripture, and make a decision. Your view about hell is foundational to your beliefs. Please record your thoughts, your questions, and any other Scriptures that come to mind below as you seek to understand the truth about hell.

Day 5

TURNING FROM DARKNESS

The heaviness of yesterday's lesson still lingers, and to be honest, I hope it will always linger in our hearts. The reality of hell should feed our desire not only to submit our own lives to Christ but also to share His love with others. The amazing truth is there is HOPE for us all! Yes, there is separation from God, His holiness, and His light for those who don't follow Him, but for those who repent, turn from their sin, and turn to Jesus for salvation, there is life! When we cry out to Him, He saves us.

Consider one pastor's definition of darkness: "There is no distance in darkness. Darkness is limitation, darkness is imprisonment; there is no jail with walls so thick and impenetrable as darkness."[9] As you read Psalm 107:8–16, keep this visual picture of darkness being a prison and reflect on how only Jesus can set us free.

From verses 10–11, what caused people to sit in darkness, bound in chains?

....

....

What did they have to do to turn from darkness? (verse 13)

....

....

How did the Lord respond to their cries? (verses 14 and 16)

What should our response be when He delivers us? (verse 15)

This is a beautiful Scripture depicting the amazing truth of our salvation. We were all once bound in chains of death and sat in a state of darkness and affliction. Yet there was a moment when you recognized your sin and you cried out to God. You acknowledged Jesus as your Savior, asked Him to save you, and He did! He broke through the chains of death and delivered you out of the darkness.

Romans 10:9 says, "If you confess with your mouth that Jesus is Lord and believe in your heart that God raised him from the dead, you will be saved." This is the astonishing truth: it's simple. Crying out involves humbling ourselves, recognizing the Lord as the only God and Savior, and giving Him our lives. He is just waiting to hear our voices calling out in submission to Him. Then He brings us out of the darkness and breaks the chains of death.

There is another beautiful Scripture I want you to look at. Please copy Isaiah 42:6–7 below:

The "you" in this verse is singular, which means it is referring to one particular individual. In the first four verses from this chapter, the "you" is clarified as "my servant" and "my chosen" who will "bring forth justice." Who are these verses referring to?

Later, in verse 16, God says, "And I will lead the blind in a way that they do not know, in paths that they have not known I will guide them. I will turn the darkness before them into light, the rough places into level ground. These are the things I do, and I do not forsake them." God's promises are true! He has given us Jesus as the light to the nations and will turn the darkness into light.

A beautiful portrayal of this is the literal way in which Jesus brought sight. Turn to the New Testament and read all of John 9.

What reason did Jesus give that this man was born blind?

____

____

How did Jesus demonstrate His power to heal both physically and spiritually?

____

____

Jesus provides sight—not only physically sight but spiritual sight. He is the Light, the one who has the power to heal us of all our diseases and of all our sins. Though this week was difficult and heavy, we have hope! Don't end this week in fear or discouragement. Finish in knowing that you have the Light, and He has set you free from darkness. Praise Him for all He has done and His power over the darkness! "The Lord is my light and my salvation; whom shall I fear?" (Psalm 27:1)

Week 3:
The Purpose of Light

Day 1

SHINING THROUGH US

Thus far, we've looked at our source of light and darkness. This week, we will be studying the purpose of light. As we've read in John 9:5, Jesus said, "As long as I am in the world, I am the light of the world." Yet it's been about two thousand years since Jesus walked this earth. So where is the light now?

Matthew 5 is a very rich Scripture. It begins with one of Jesus's most well-known sermons, the Beatitudes. Then, Jesus continues to teach in what is called the Similitudes. It's interesting to note that "similitude" means "the quality or state of being similar to something; a comparison between two things."[10] This is where our key verses are found. Take note of the two things being compared.

Record Matthew 5:14–16 below:

....

....

....

....

What is Jesus comparing us to?

....

....

To whom are we to be a light?

What is the purpose of our light?

This is an astounding truth: We are the light! I don't want you to miss how significant this is. In the book of John, Jesus makes seven "I am" statements to define his identity, but only one does He declare about us too. Read through those statements below:

1. I am the Bread of Life. (John 6:35)
2. I am the Light of the World. (John 8:12)
3. I am the Door. (John 10:7)
4. I am the Good Shepherd. (John 10:11)
5. I am the Resurrection and the Life. (John 11:25)
6. I am the Way, Truth, and the Life. (John 14:6)
7. I am the Vine. (John 15:5)

All of these statements are unique to the identity of Jesus. Yet He also gave us the privilege of being lights of the world. We now have a purpose and a mission to be lights just as Jesus is the Light.

I'm going to ask you an initial question with the hope that your answer will change, be added to, and be deepened by the end of this study. At this point, what does it mean to you to be a light to the world?

Now read 1 Thessalonians 5:4–5. How are we described in these verses?

A child is a reflection of his or her birth parents. As God's children, we are reflections of His light. In order to reflect God correctly, it is necessary to understand the purposes of light. This week, we'll look at three purposes of light. However, all these purposes lead to a single goal. Do you know what that goal is? Isaiah 49:6 says, "I will make you as a light for the nations, that my salvation may reach to the end of the earth."

For whom are we to be a light, and why?

Paul repeats this Scripture when he speaks to the gentiles in Acts 13:47–48. Read these verses and answer the questions below.

Who gave this command to Paul?

Again, what is the purpose of "his" light?

Now, the gentiles were "everyone else," anyone who wasn't a Jew. The Jewish people were originally the chosen people who received God's truth, but God made it available to everyone else. Most of us fit into this gentile category. Let's not skip over the beautiful way the gentiles responded to this statement by Paul.

Record how the gentiles respond in verse 48:

Oh, what joy these Antioch gentiles had! Can you relate? God has given His salvation to all people: rich, poor, black, white, Jewish, gentile. All can receive salvation. Titus 2:11 says, "For the grace of God has appeared, bringing salvation for all people." What an awesome truth we can rejoice in!

How does this purpose relate to you? The fact is that you are the light, and you are to bring salvation to the ends of the earth. How this looks will be different for each of us, and my prayer is that you'll identify how God is using you, or wants to use you, in the upcoming weeks. As we discuss the purposes of light during this week, don't forget the ultimate goal: that His salvation would be made known to all people for His glory!

Day 2

REVEALING THE WAY

Light works in multiple ways to bring about salvation. We'll discuss three of those methods throughout this week, starting with how light reveals the way. Just as a physical light reveals the way ahead of us, God's truth illuminates the darkness to reveal the way to salvation in Jesus Christ. And just as Jesus's light reveals the way, we as lights can also reveal the truth to others. In order for us to understand how we can do this, let's first look at how God and Jesus reveal the way.

Throughout the events recorded in the Old Testament, God revealed Himself to people in various ways. One example is how God led the people of Israel. Read Exodus 13:21–22 and Deuteronomy 1:32–33. How did God lead the people of Israel and for what purpose?

____

____

God led the people of Israel to safety, to a good place—to a land He promised them. God revealed His Shekinah glory. In other words, His glorious presence was manifested in a visible way and lit the way before them. In the New Testament, Jesus revealed the way to Paul using a similar method.

Turn to Acts 26:12–18. Read this account of Paul's encounter with Jesus, and then answer the following questions:

How did Jesus appear to Paul?

What was Paul sent to do?

Do you see the cause and effect? First, the light of God (or Jesus) reveals His way to His people, and then they have the opportunity to respond in obedience by going in the direction He has revealed to them. Paul recognizes this in Galatians 1:15–16 when he says, "But when he who had set me apart before I was born, and who called me by his grace, was pleased to reveal his Son to me, in order that I might preach him among the Gentiles . . ."

Can you think of ways that God has revealed His way to you? Record some examples below.

Today, God may not reveal Himself to you through a burning bush, a cloud of fire, or a blinding light (though He could). However, He does reveal His way to us through His Word, through prayer, and by speaking to us through the Holy Spirit. The fact is that God is not limited in how He reveals Himself, and He often does it unexpectedly.

God also uses other believers to reveal Himself and share His salvation. Look at Peter in Acts 2:38–41. How many were saved that day through Peter's teaching?

Now, if you are like me, you are not necessarily an evangelist like Peter. However, there are many ways in which we can reveal God's truth to people. Think about what this means to you individually. In what ways can you reveal the way to others?

....

....

....

Revealing the way goes hand in hand with Christ's command in Matthew 28:19-20: "Go therefore and make disciples of all nations, baptizing them in the name of the Father and of the Son and of the Holy Spirit, teaching them to observe all that I have commanded you. And behold, I am with you always, to the end of the age."

List the verbs in these verses:

....

....

All of these verbs are involved in being a light. We need to go, make, baptize, and teach. We usually hear this verse at missions conferences, calling people to the remote parts of the world, but that isn't its only meaning. Yes, you may be asked to go to a foreign country, but you're more likely to be called to be a light to the people who are around you now: neighbors, coworkers, those who are in need nearby, friends, and family. However, don't forget that going involves making disciples, teaching, and baptizing. That means it's not just about an invitation to a single prayer. It's about the time-intensive, walking-alongside-someone act of discipleship. We are to be disciples—teaching, showing by example, and doing life together. That is how we will reveal the way to those in darkness.

At this point, can you name people to whom the Lord has directed you to reveal His light? If you can't name anybody, take the time to ask God whom He would like you to go to and disciple, and record the name(s) below.

Next turn to Romans 10:13–15 and answer the following questions:

Who will be saved?

How will people believe?

You may be thinking that these verses don't apply to you because you aren't a preacher or a "sent" missionary. But God has called all of His disciples (you and me) to be His light and to partner in the ministry of bringing salvation. In fact, the shoes of peace that bring good news are part of the spiritual armor we are supposed to put on in Ephesians 6:15. As Isaiah 52:7 says,

> How beautiful upon the mountains
>   are the feet of him who brings good news,
> who publishes peace, who brings good news of happiness,
>   who publishes salvation,
>   who says to Zion, "Your God reigns."

The words from this verse fill me with joy—"beautiful," "good," "peace," "happiness"! What about you? How do these verses make you feel? My prayer today is that you would be filled with joy as you understand more of the purpose that God has for you in bringing His good news to those who are in darkness by revealing the way to eternal life through salvation in Jesus Christ.

Day 3

EXPOSING SIN—PART 1

How many of you have the pleasure of living in an area with cockroaches? If you live in the southern states, Africa, Asia, or one of many other places around the world, you understand the behavior of cockroaches. You see, cockroaches love to hide in dark places and only come out at night. Here in Uganda, they love to hide under our bathtubs. I can't see them during the day. I wouldn't even know they were there. However, at night, after all the lights go out, they come out of their hiding places. I try to avoid going to the bathroom at night, because I know what I'm going to find. As soon as I switch on the light, I'll see several cockroaches scurrying for cover as the light exposes them. If I'm quick enough, I can doom them before they run to safety.

These cockroaches remind me of sin. Sin loves to hide in the darkness and runs from the light. However, light is a powerful tool used to expose sin. For some, this is a scary thought, because we don't want our sin exposed. But the reality is that our sin is never hidden from God. It's only hidden from others—and sometimes even from ourselves. God knows all that is secret and hidden. Write out the following verses:

Psalm 90:8

____

____

____

Proverbs 20:27

1 Corinthians 4:5

According to these verses, how does God expose our sin?

Okay, personal question. In the past, how has God exposed your sin through His light?

Luke 12:2–3 says, "Nothing is covered up that will not be revealed, or hidden that will not be known. Therefore whatever you have said in the dark shall be heard in the light, and what you have whispered in private rooms shall be proclaimed on the housetops." The key word here is "nothing." Nothing will remain hidden, and all that is in darkness will be revealed. You see, we can't hide from God, and any sin we think we have hidden really isn't. That's another one of Satan's lies: our sin won't be found out.

Okay, now a question about the present. Is there a sin that you think you are hiding and need to confess? Tough question, I know! But be honest with yourself and with others, because the truth is that God already knows.

Not only does light expose our own sin, but it's also used to expose the sins of those around us. Let's look at Scripture to gain insight on how we can walk in the light in a way that exposes sin. Go ahead and read all of Ephesians 5:1–14.

In this passage, there are four aspects of being a light that work together to expose sin. The first aspect is that we are to *live out the fruits of light.* Fruit is produced when you are attached to the vine, Jesus. Read John 15:1–8. What is necessary to produce fruit?

____

____

As we abide in Christ, the fruits of the Spirit will naturally reveal themselves in our lives. So what specifically are the fruits of light? Some are listed here, and the other fruits of the Spirit are listed in Galatians 5:22–25. Use these verses to list the fruits of walking in the light:

____

____

____

How do you think living out the fruits of the Holy Spirit works to expose sin?

____

____

Fruit is the part of character and behavior that is visible to others. In his commentary on Ephesians, R. K. Hughes says, "When the light of Jesus is refracted through the prisms of our lives, there will be sanctifying shades of life for others to see. We then 'find out what pleases the Lord,' and so do others."[11] Back when I was a sixth-grade teacher, we studied light as part of a science unit. One of my favorite activities was to take a prism and hold it at the perfect angle for the light to go through and be refracted into a beautiful rainbow. That is what living out the fruits of light entails. It's a brilliant display of Jesus's light for all to see as we angle our lives toward Jesus.

The second aspect is to *take no part in the unfruitful works of darkness* (verse 11). List some of the unfruitful works mentioned in verses 3–7:

These works accomplish the exact opposite of the fruitful works we are to walk in. There is no fruit or value in them. Now, I want you to notice something. It says that we are not to have fellowship with the "works" of the darkness. It doesn't say that we are not to fellowship with people who sin (which is impossible!). What do you think it means to have no fellowship with their works?

Do you remember when we discussed 2 Corinthians 6:14 and how we are not to be "yoked to unbelievers?" Ephesians 5:7 says something similar: "Therefore do not become partners with them." Again, the importance of not being attached to a nonbeliever or their works is the key. We are to live life among nonbelievers, but just because we are around them doesn't mean that we are to be participants in the evil works they do.

The third aspect of exposing sin is that *we are not to even speak of the works of darkness* (verses 4 and 12). We are to physically stay away from the works of darkness and mentally keep them from our minds by not discussing them. There is a time to call out someone's sin (we'll discuss that tomorrow), as well as a time to ask for prayer when struggling with a particular sin, but that is not what this verse is referring to. This verse is speaking about the morbid curiosity and interest that leads us to talk about sin and the evil that people do. Like they say in the news world, sin sells. It's the bloody, scandalous, and horrifying that captures people's attention. This should not be the case for those that walk in the light. Earlier, in Ephesians 4:29, Paul says, "Let no corrupting talk come out of your mouths, but only such as is good for building up, as fits the occasion, that it may give grace to those who hear." What are the two things that our words should do?

1) ____

2) ____

When we discuss sinful things, does that accomplish these two things?

____

The fourth aspect of being a light is that *we expose sin.* As we walk according to these verses, our light will shine forth and will naturally expose what is around us. What do verses 13 and 14 say becomes of anything that is exposed by the light?

____

____

Light has the power to make things visible, and not only that but actually has the ability to turn things into light. The word "expose" can also be translated as "convince," which seems to work in this context as "the person who is exposed and convinced by the light is transformed."[12] As our light shines forth, those who are exposed have the opportunity to receive the light and become light themselves. This is our mission—to expose what was once in darkness to the light of Jesus.

Day 4

EXPOSING SIN—PART 2

My kids love to play with flashlights. But inevitably, one of them will "accidently" shine their beam of light into another person's eyes, temporarily blinding them and making them turn away. Now, remember our lives are meant to shine into others to expose their sin so that they repent and turn to Jesus. However, we can be like my six-year-old's flashlight and shine so directly, carelessly, and extremely that we cause someone to turn away from the light. I'm sure you can think of examples of how people were blinded by a Christian or multiple Christians shining too brightly or in the wrong way. Write down an example, either a personal experience or a story you heard, below.

What a tragedy when God's people actually cause someone to turn away from God instead of drawing them to Him. I can think of several Scriptures that reveal characteristics of a blinding light. Look them up and write down the blinding behavior in these verses:

Matthew 6:1–6

Matthew 7:1–5

Mark 7:1–9

Luke 11:37–42

Notice that many of these verses involve or address the Pharisees. Now, the Pharisees were the religious leaders, though they led in hypocrisy. They demanded the utmost obedience to their Jewish laws, yet their hearts were far from God. We become harmful lights when we become like those Pharisees—casting judgment (without love), thinking we are better than others, caring more about traditions than the heart, wanting praise and accolades, and confronting sin without humbleness.

Though we can't change others' actions, we can look at ourselves and work at shining in the right way. First, remember we are all sinners. "ALL fall short of the glory of God" (Romans 3:23). Second, even though we are called to expose sin, we are not called to judge sin. That's God's role. Psalm 96:13 says, "For he comes to judge the earth. He will judge the world in righteousness, and the peoples in faithfulness."

What do you think is the difference between judging sin and exposing sin?

The way you live your life will often prompt the conviction in another person's life, as discussed in day 3. However, when you are called to confront someone about their sin, there is a correct way to do so.

Read 2 Timothy 2:23–26. What does it say to avoid?

How are we to confront someone?

What may be the result of us correcting in the right way?

Notice that it is God who has the ability to grant repentance, not us. That is the work of the Holy Spirit. We have the opportunity to pave the way for the Holy Spirit to work with our kindness, patience, and gentleness. As we conduct ourselves in this way, our opponents have a chance to "come to their senses" which can also be translated as "to become sober again."

Later, in 2 Timothy 4:2, Paul charges Timothy to "preach the word; be ready in season and out of season; reprove, rebuke, and exhort, with complete patience and teaching." Those last words are the key: "with complete patience and teaching." We can't just rebuke or reprove someone without teaching him or her along the way in the most patient and gentle manner. Teaching takes time, and again, this goes back to discipleship. It means you are involved in the person's life and invested in them.

Turn to Galatians 6:1. How does this verse tell us to confront someone?

Take note of the warning in this verse. How could you be tempted when restoring someone who is in sin?

You may have answered that last question with how you could fall into the same sin as the one you are restoring. That is sometimes true. However, I also want to caution you that often the temptation we face in correcting someone is pride. How easy it is to feel superior to the person you are confronting. Before we confront, we should always check our motives to make sure there is no feeling of superiority. We need to "humble ourselves before the Lord," as James 4:10 says. The Pharisees conducted themselves in pride and arrogance. To avoid becoming blinding lights, we must be alert for those same sins in ourselves.

I want you to really ponder this. What do these verses mean to you? Are you being asked to confront someone in a gentle, humble way? Or is the Lord convicting you of being a "blinding" light, so you need to ask someone's forgiveness for confronting them in the wrong way? Please spend the last few minutes searching your heart and asking the Lord to reveal any names of people to you.

____

____

____

Day 5

DRAWING OTHERS

As I write this, I'm sitting on a veranda overlooking Lake Victoria in Uganda. The lake is not only majestic but a source of income for many people. At night, you can look out over the water and see dozens of little lights. These lights are lanterns hung on the boats of nighttime fishermen. However, the lights aren't there so that the fishermen can see what they are doing. They are there to attract the fish. Schools of little tiny silver fish are attracted to the light, and as they come up to the surface to get closer to the light, the fishermen can catch them. We also need to be an attractive light, one that draws people to it and then "captures" them with God's love.

I love the following verses from Isaiah. In fact, this is the passage that captured my heart to write this study. Read Isaiah 60:1–3 below:

> Arise, shine, for your light has come,
> and the glory of the Lord has risen upon you.
> For behold, darkness shall cover the earth,
> and thick darkness the peoples;
> but the Lord will arise upon you,
> and His glory will be seen upon you.
> And nations shall come to your light,
> and kings to the brightness of your rising.

How does this verse describe the earth and the peoples of the earth?

How does this verse describe God's light in "you"?

Who will be drawn to your light?

How does knowing that His glory will be seen upon you make you feel?

The "you" in these verses is referring to the city of Zion, revealed later in verse 14. Yet this is not Jerusalem as it was known in Isaiah's time, nor as we know it now. This is the New Jerusalem (Revelation 21), where all believers will be gathered. You are a part of that city; you are a part of the church today that will reveal God's glorious light and draw nations to Him. God's glory, as seen in you, will attract those who are in darkness.

Keeping with the fisherman analogy, turn to Matthew 4:18–22. What did Jesus call these fishermen to do?

What do you think it means to be "fishers of men"?

How can we draw others to us? Let's read the following Scriptures and record what characteristics would be attractive to others.

Matthew 5:43–48

John 13:34–35

Ephesians 4:32

Titus 3:1–2

Christ is our example. As He loved, we are to love. As He drew people to Himself, so we are to draw people to us and ultimately to Him. During His three years of ministry, Jesus constantly had hordes of people following Him. In fact, many times, people had to go to extreme measures just to get to Jesus. Remember the story of Zacchaeus, the "wee little man" who had to climb a tree to see Jesus? Jesus invited Himself to Zacchaeus's house, where Zacchaeus repented. In response Jesus told him, "Today salvation has come to this house, because he also is a son of Abraham; for the Son of Man has come to seek and to save that which was lost" (Luke 19:9–10).

Who did Jesus come to save? The lost! Go ahead and read Mark 2:13–17 and Luke 15:1–2. What kinds of people were drawn to Jesus?

This is important for us to remember. It was the sinners, those who needed a savior, who were drawn to Jesus. Our love is meant to draw sinners to Jesus. I pray that our faith and the way we live our lives are attractive to the people around us, that we lure them in with the love of Jesus and capture them with His saving grace.

This week, we looked at the purposes of light. Always remember that the ultimate purpose of light is to make known His salvation to all people for His glory! We do this by revealing the way to salvation, exposing sin, and drawing people to Jesus. Let's arise and shine, dear sisters, so those who are in darkness will come into His glorious light!

Week 4:

The Hidden Light

Day 1

WHERE IS THE LIGHT?

Electricity is not reliable where I live in Northern Uganda. It turns off several times a week, sometimes for a few hours, sometimes for days. And of course, it always turns off right when you need it. One particular night, my husband had left to drive some visitors home after dinner. I was in the process of cleaning up and getting my five kids bathed and ready for bed. It had already been a hectic evening, and bedtime couldn't come soon enough. Suddenly, the lights went out, and we were thrown into darkness. Chaos ensued immediately as five children started screaming, a huge thud came from the shower followed by crying, and I frantically groped in the dark for our solar lights. I needed a light to illuminate the darkness so I could help my children and save them from harm. The need for light was great. Why would I then proceed to find the solar light in the windowsill, turn it on, and then hide the light?

The reality is this is often what we do. The need is great! There are people hurting, screaming for help, and floundering in the darkness. Yet the light that we have, we hide. Why? List some reasons you think we hide our light:

____

____

____

We've already discussed how we are the light of the world and looked at Matthew 5:14–16. Now, turn to the corresponding Scriptures in Mark and Luke. Write down these verses below and highlight (or underline) the ways in which lights are hidden.

Mark 4:21

Luke 8:16

If we are meant to be a light (or lamp), what would that mean for us if we are not?

A ball is meant to bounce. A car is meant to be driven. A light is meant to shine. When we are not doing what we are meant to do, a lot of issues arise. We can feel lost and without purpose or question our identity in Christ. All of these heart issues can be related to not fulfilling the role God has given us. What happens to a light that is put under something? It dies out because it doesn't have oxygen. When we hide our light, the same thing happens to us. Our faith dies out because it is lacking the oxygen that keeps it ignited. What would you consider "oxygen" to your faith?

Hiding our light not only has implications for ourselves but also severely affects others. Remember how at the beginning of this study we discussed that this world seems to be getting darker? Well, that is what happens when light is hidden; when light is hidden, things go dark.

Over the next week, we'll look at the reasons we hide our light. Please trust me when I say that we all struggle in one way or another with hiding our lights. It can be intentional or unintentional, but hiding is something that everyone has to fight against. Though each of us has individual reasons to hide, the overarching reason is fear. Fear is the cover that we hide under. It's the tool that Satan uses to keep our light from shining out in the darkness. Fear not only immobilizes us but prevents us from fulfilling our purpose. Let's go to the Lord this week and look at the reasons we hide and why we fear. Spend the last few minutes today evaluating your own life to see if you are shining or hiding. If you are hiding, ask God why. Go before Him in prayer and listen to what He has to say. Write down any thoughts, prayers, or words from God below.

____

____

____

____

Day 2

WHAT DO WE FEAR?

What are the fears that keep you from being a light? What hinders you from shining in a way that reveals who God is, exposes sin, and draws others to Jesus? I hope that yesterday God revealed some things to you.

There are many fears that we face: death, sickness, loss of a loved one, catastrophe, etc. However, the fear most prevalent in preventing us from shining is the fear of man. The fear of man comes in many shapes and sizes. We can fear what people think of us or what they'll do to us. We fear embarrassment, being ridiculed, or having others think we are ignorant. We may even say we don't want to offend or seem judgmental. These are all relevant fears that we need to address and examine in our lives.

Fear is a tool that Satan uses to incapacitate us, to prevent our light from shining. If we allow it, fear can dictate our decisions and be a stumbling block in the work God has for us to do. Proverbs 29:25 says, "The fear of man lays a snare, but whoever trusts in the Lord is safe." Imagine a snare, or a trap, that grabs your legs and makes you immobile. You aren't able to do what the Lord has asked you to do or go where He has asked you to go. That is what happens when we fear men. Allowing fear to hinder what the Lord has for us is all too common. In fact, it happened to multiple men and women in the Bible. Let's take a look at two of them, the first being Saul at the beginning of his reign.

Read 1 Samuel 10:17–27.

Who dictated who would be king?

Why do you think Saul hid?

Now, before these verses, Samuel had spoken to Saul about God's will for him to be king (verse 1). Even though he had the Lord's blessing, Saul still feared. He may have feared the crowd, what people thought, or even rejection, which actually happened. Verse 27 says some rebels despised him and said, "How can this man save us?" Saul would continue to let fear dictate his decisions when he later tried to kill David after realizing that David would replace him as king.

Think how differently Saul's life would have been without fear driving him. He could have ruled with authority and confidence, knowing it was God who put him in charge. Yet instead of living in submission to God's will, Saul let fear turn him away from the Lord. Saul even admitted his fear in 1 Samuel 15:24 after he disobeyed God by making a sacrifice himself instead of waiting for Samuel the priest. He said, "I have sinned, for I have transgressed the commandment of the Lord and your words, because I feared the people and obeyed their voice."

In the verse above, underline or highlight who Saul feared.

Next, let's take a look at a New Testament character, Simon Peter. Peter truly loved the Lord and served as his disciple for many years. Yet he, too, allowed fear to dictate his decisions and made a grievous mistake. Read Matthew 26:69–75 and answer the following questions:

What did Peter fear?

What did his fears lead him to do?

As heartbreaking as this was for Peter, he was able to see Jesus again, and his faith was restored. In fact, henceforth he fervently served God with his entire life, even unto death.

For you and I, these Scriptures can serve as both a warning and an encouragement. We will fail, just like Peter and Saul did, but God is faithful and true to forgive and to restore our faith. Don't be like Saul, who continued to live in fear and allowed it to rule his life, leading to his eventual downfall. Learn from Peter, who turned from fear to complete trust in God, and who God used mightily.

Can you relate to these men? Think of a time you allowed fear to cause you to turn away from doing what God called you to do or to not stand up for what you believe in. Write your story below.

Let's look at what God says about the fear of man. Write down the following two verses:

Psalm 118:6

1 Peter 3:13–14

What do you think the question "What can man do to me?" implies?

Many Scriptures about fear tell us how we will be kept safe, free from harm, or even blessed. Is that really true? If you trust in the Lord, will you always be safe?

Difficult question because the answer is yes and no. No in the fact that we still live in this broken world where we will face sickness, death, and tragedies. Even more so, as you stand up for what is right, you are almost guaranteed to be ridiculed and isolated, to lose relationships, status, jobs, and even in some countries your freedom or life. But despite facing these things, YES, He will keep us safe. God promises something so much better than what we would ever lose. He promises Himself. He promises blessing and the incredible hope of a future after this life. For the eternal future, in God's glorious presence we are safe and secure. Nothing can harm our souls.

Let's look at one more Scripture today, Jeremiah 17:5–8. Read those verses before answering the following questions:

What warning is given to those who trust in man?

What blessing is given to those who trust in the Lord?

The problem with fear is that not only does it incapacitate us to do God's work, but it means we aren't trusting in God. Do you trust that God will protect you, strengthen you, and provide all that you need, regardless of what people do or say?"

Can you think of a time you allowed God to be your strength and were able to conquer your fear of people? If you have a story, record it below.

I remember a particular time when, during a church service, the Spirit prompted me to pray for a certain woman that was sitting on the opposite side of the sanctuary. I didn't know her. I didn't know what she needed prayer for or if she was a believer. But I did know that He wanted me to pray for her—and not just pray on my own, but physically walk up to her and pray with her. I was terrified. I mean, this was possibly a fellow sister in Christ, but she was a complete stranger to me, and who knew what she would think of me? I was so worried about what she would think that I almost didn't go. But I finally did, and it was such a blessing, for her and for me. Please understand that most of us struggle with fearing what people will think, say, or do. I pray that we can all step out in faith, uncover our light from this fear, and move forward in what God asks us to do.

Day 3

YOU WILL BE HATED

Recognizing our fear can be hard. However, my hope is that you are encouraged in the fact that even the strongest of believers face fear. God has promised to never leave us, and we can trust that He will restore us when we fail. Today, we have to ask ourselves a very difficult question. Are you ready? Here is the question: Are you willing to be hated? Yikes! Wait, wait, wait! I bet you are saying to yourselves, "That's a contradiction! First, we are to draw others to us by being an attractive light to them, and now, we should be okay with being hated by the very people we are to draw to us? Which is it?" It's okay if that is what you are thinking. Let me explain, and of course, let's look at what the Word of God says.

The reality is that if you are a light and you stand up for what you believe, you won't always be liked. There will be people who hate you, who tell you that you're judgmental, and who ridicule you for what you believe. 2 Corinthians 2:15–16 says, "For we are the aroma of Christ to God among those who are being saved and among those who are perishing, to one a fragrance from death to death, to the other a fragrance from life to life. Who is sufficient for these things?"

Are you adequate for this task—to be the smell of death to some and life to others?

....

....

That's a super tough question! Even as I write this study, I'm thinking about how I don't want to cause offense. I worry about coming off as judgmental. I hope people like me. Did you notice the key word in those sentences? "I." When we are thinking about ourselves, we are not thinking about God and what He has asked us to do. This will lead us to hide our light or share it incorrectly, using our own means and methods. When we allow Christ to shine through us, those self-doubts go away, and it's not about us. When people reject us, they are actually rejecting Christ. So when they hate you, they are hating their Creator and Lord.

Can you think of a time you have been hated for believing in Jesus? (This can also come in the form of being ridiculed, ostracized, or put down because of your faith.) Record your story below:

Next, take a look at the following verses and write down what each verse is telling you.

Matthew 10:22

Luke 6:22

1 John 3:13

Did you catch that? We aren't to be surprised that the world hates us! We should actually expect it. And for whose sake are we to be hated and reviled?

____

Now, drawing people to us isn't about being popular, making sure everyone feels accepted, or being okay with the sin people commit. We are to draw people to the TRUTH, not some false prosperity, feel-good gospel that just makes everyone happy. That would be lying and leading people to hell, not Jesus. Remember, Jesus is our light and reference point. He loved all people, yet He always pointed to the truth, and for this He was hated.

Give some examples of how Jesus was hated because He upheld the truth:

____

____

Jesus always gave glory to His Father in all that He said and did, even when He was upturning tables, chastising the Pharisees, and calling out sin. He knew that the only way for people to find true life, the only way to truly love people, was to reveal their sin so that they would repent and turn to God. The most loving thing we can do for people is give them the truth of God's Word and His salvation, and unfortunately, that may mean people hate us. Galatians 1:10 says, "For am I now seeking the approval of man, or of God? Or am I trying to please man? If I were still trying to please man, I would not be a servant of Christ."

Personal question: Are you trying to please people or God?

____

____

Of course, we want to do this in the right way and avoid being a blinding light like we discussed previously, but our goal isn't to win a popularity contest. Our goal is to lead people to Jesus in order to bring Him glory.

Take the time to read 2 Corinthians 6:4–10 and then specifically record 2 Corinthians 6:8:

Will you and I do this? Will you serve God whether people honor you or despise you? I know this is a tough lesson. Spend a few minutes reflecting on this question and record your thoughts below.

Day 4

GOD'S LOVE CASTS OUT FEAR

Now that we have identified the fear that prevents our light from shining forth, how do we conquer that fear? LOVE! God's love in our lives releases us from fears, anxiety, and worry—all that would prevent us from being a light for Him. Over the next two days, we'll look at how God's love casts aside our fear as we love Him and love others.

1 John 4 is such a rich text on God's love and how it transforms us. Please go ahead and read 1 John 4:7–21 before answering the following questions:

How has the love of God been demonstrated to you?

____

____

How can we be perfected in love? (Hint: also look at 1 John 2:4–6)

____

____

What do you think it means that "there is no fear in love"?

____

____

"Beloved"—such an endearing word—is used twice in this passage to identify the church, which includes you and me. We are beloved, loved by God. Do you fully believe this amazing truth? Because not until we believe that God loves us can we be released from fear. He loved us first, unconditionally, and even without us returning His love. Romans 8:38–39 says, "For I am sure that neither death nor life, nor angels nor rulers, nor things present nor things to come, nor powers, nor height nor depth, nor anything else in all of creation, will be able to separate us from the love of God in Christ Jesus our Lord." There are no strings attached to His love. There is nothing we can do to earn it, to keep it, or to get rid of it. It's as Martin Luther said: "God does not love because of our works; He loves because of His love."[13]

What prevents you from believing in God's unconditional love for you?

Now just to clarify, the specific fear being addressed in 1 John 4 is the fear of God's coming judgment. The ultimate fear that we face is death and facing a holy awesome God. Yet because of God's great love for us, we have "boldness in the day of judgment." Jesus said in John 5:24, "Whoever hears my word and believes him who sent me has eternal life. He does not come into judgment." Since we have this assurance, we are freed from fear, all fears, because all other fears fall under this overarching fear of the unknown future and all fears are covered by His love.

What kind of emotions result from fear? Anxiety, worry, anger, and shame. God tells us to trust Him, "casting all your anxieties on him, because he cares for you" (1 Peter 5:7). In other words, "Do not worry or fear, because He loves you!" This may be something that you struggle with: believing that God cares for you. Look up and record the following verses in order to grasp more of His care and provision:

Matthew 7:11

Romans 8:15

James 1:17

When you are given the freedom to call God "Abba Father," and you know that He's given you good gifts, does that create trust and relieve you of fear?

Look back at today's first Scripture, 1 John 4:7–21. From these verses, what should our response to God's love be?

We love Him back, and we love others! We'll discuss loving others tomorrow, but loving God involves abiding in His love, trusting Him, and following His commands. As we abide, we trust in His goodness and walk in obedience, knowing that whatever happens, He is in control and taking care of us. Remember when we discussed Jesus submitting to the cross? Jesus said, "But I do as the Father has commanded me, so that the world may know that I love the Father" (John 14:31). Jesus revealed His love through His obedience, and we have the opportunity to do the same.

In fact, God actually "commands" us to love Him in return. Let's look at two coordinating Scriptures, Deuteronomy 6:5 and Matthew 22:36–40. I know many of you could say these Scriptures from memory, but I want you to look at them with fresh eyes. What does it mean to love God with all your heart, soul, and might?

A commandment is similar to a rule. It is an instruction given that you must follow; otherwise, there will be consequences. Think of other commandments in Deuteronomy: Do not murder. Do not steal. Most people would agree to such rules and obey them. Yet it's hard to consider "Love God" to be a rule. Why do you think God commanded us to love Him?

God knows us better than we know ourselves. He knows our sinful hearts and wayward ways. We are like children that need to be told what to do over and over again. He also knows that this command is something that we not only should do, but need to do. That it is for our best! Because when we love the Lord with everything that we are, everything that we have, our ALL, then all other things fall away. The fears that you have, the fears that I have, all fall away as we love God. Loving God also means that you love the things He loves—people, this world, and His creation. And you aren't worried about popularity, money, or what people think of you. In other words, you don't care about what the world cares about—you care about what God cares about.

You may think if we are commanded, we don't have a choice, so it's not really love. But we always have a choice and will face the consequences of that choice. However, if we truly trust in God's unfailing love for us and His goodness, then we can trust that His commands are for our best. Loving the Lord in this way casts aside the fears of this world. This world, the people living in it, the evil that exists in it will not have a hold on us, and we will do anything that the Lord asks, because we love Him.

Remember, dear sister, "God gave us a spirit not of fear but of power and love and self-control" (2 Timothy 1:7).

When I allow the Lord to pour His love over me, the worries, fears, and anxiety of this life fall away. So I want you to spend the last few minutes of this study basking in God's love for you. Read this beautiful quote from Spurgeon and meditate on how much God loves YOU!

> Who is it that loves you? God, the Maker of heaven and earth, the Almighty, All in all, does He love me? Even He? If all men, and all angels, and all the living creatures that are before the throne loved me, it were nothing to this—the Infinite loves me! And who is it that He loves? *Me.* The text saith, "us." "We love Him because He first loved us." But this is the personal point—He loves me, an insignificant nobody, full of sin— who deserved to be in hell; who loves Him so little in return—God loves ME."[14]

____

____

____

____

Day 5

LOVE (OF PEOPLE) CASTS OUT FEAR

I have a sweet friend, Filder, who helps me in my Ugandan home. She is a godly woman and excels at having a gentle and quiet spirit. Today, however, she wasn't so quiet as her voice rang out, shouting at me to come to the window from where I sat at the dining room table, homeschooling my children. When I looked out the window, she pointed to a snake crouched at our door. Now, I am terrified of snakes, which is a legitimate fear for a mom living in Africa. My fear would normally cause me to turn and run the other way. However, since the snake posed a threat to those I loved, I armed myself with a baseball bat and a machete, preparing to kill it. Thankfully, sensing danger, the snake quickly slithered away and escaped through a hole in the wall before I had a chance to get too close. Even though I was scared, my love for my children cast aside my fear and caused me to act in order to protect them.

There are many stories out there of people who overcame their fear to save their loved ones. I'm sure you can even think of a time when you've cast aside your fear because of your love. When we love people, there are times we do what we thought we couldn't do, what we fear to do, to save them.

Let me ask you something: do you love people? We're not just talking about those you naturally love, like your family and friends; we are talking about the whole world. Do you love the people of this world enough to save them? Because that is what God asks us to do—save their lives from sin and darkness and bring them into the wonderful salvation of our Lord Jesus Christ.

We'll refer back to yesterday's readings, first looking again at Matthew 22:36–40. What is the second-greatest commandment? Write it down below:

Next, return to 1 John 4:7–21 and look specifically for the phrase that is repeated in verses 7, 11, and 12. What is that phrase?

Remember, John is speaking to the church in 1 John, so we can easily say "loving one another" is inclusive of loving our brothers and sisters in Christ, as further seen in 4:20–5:2. However, if we are to love as He has loved us (verse 11), our model is Christ, who died for all people. "The Father has sent his Son to be the Savior of the world" (verse 17). As Leon Morris writes in *Testaments of Love*, "This being the case, our love cannot be limited to the saved but must include all people, believers or not."[15]

Loving people God's way looks a lot different from loving the world's way. The world's love is dependent on what the return is—love, gifts, wealth, praise, etc.—but God's love is unconditional, without expectation of a return, and for all people. When we love God's way, we "walk in love as Christ loved us and gave himself up for us, a fragrant offering and sacrifice to God" (Ephesians 5:2).

Let me ask you another question: What is the most loving thing we can do for the people of this world?

The most loving thing we can do for people is share the gospel with them. Caring about a person's eternal soul shows true love. I'm sure that you've heard this analogy before, but what if you had the cure to cancer? Would it be loving to withhold that cure? Of course not! Well, you hold the cure to an even more deadly disease, that of sin. The most loving thing we can do is to share Christ, the cure, with those who are dying in their sin. The significance of a person's soul going to heaven or hell for eternity is greater than that of my personal insecurities, comfort, or fears.

Even as we discuss the importance of caring for a person's spiritual needs, we can't neglect their emotional and physical needs. All these needs are intertwined in a person's well-being. Multiple verses speak to this truth.

What do the following verses tell us?

James 2:15–16

....

....

....

1 John 3:17

....

....

....

Loving someone completely involves caring about all their needs—physical, emotional, and spiritual. Of course, it is only God who can meet ALL their needs, but we can be vessels of His love in their lives and allow His Holy Spirit to work through us to help meet those needs. How do you think loving people like this works to eliminate fear? When you care more about a person's eternal future, does that take away the temporary fear of men that you may feel?

Spend the last few minutes thinking about what this means to you. I'm praying that the Lord would overwhelm you with His love, that your fears would be cast aside as you trust Him and love others, and that you (and I) would uncover our hidden light and shine forth.

Week 5:
The Unshared Light

Day 1

WHAT IS SELFISHNESS?

This week's study can sound harsh and condemning, so before we start, can I please emphasize something to you? First of all, condemnation is not of the Lord and not my intent. There is conviction, which is good, and condemnation, which is bad. Conviction is the job of the Holy Spirit. John 16:8 says, "And when he (the Holy Spirit) comes, he will convict the world concerning sin and righteousness and judgment." Yet condemnation is not from the Holy Spirit. As Romans 8:1 says, "There is therefore now no condemnation for those who are in Christ Jesus." So "I do not say this to condemn you" (2 Corinthians 7:3) but to spur you on and encourage your heart to live a life that shines for Him.

Second of all, this study is for me just as much as it is for you. I'm not about to point at the speck in your eye when I have a log in my own eye. Keeping my faith to myself is something I struggle with too. I don't want to be bothered. I'm too busy. I'm already doing "stuff" for the Lord. There are a million and one excuses. But hear me out. We are all selfish beings and come from a culture that condones selfishness. So let's take this week with grace and pray for conviction, not condemnation.

I'm sure most of us can define selfishness in our own words. *Merriam-Webster* defines the word "selfish" as "concerned excessively or exclusively with oneself: seeking or concentrating on one's own advantage, pleasure, or well-being without regard for others."[16]

This week I want to talk about spiritual selfishness. How would you define spiritual selfishness?

Think back to the very first day of the study, when we discussed the Christmas Eve service and the lighting of the candles. Remember how the candles were lit by the process of sharing the light with the person next to you? Well, what if your own candle was lit, but you didn't share it with the person next to you? Their candle would remain unlit, and so would those that were next to them. Instead of the light increasing and being shared, it would remain just a few candles lit in a dark room. This is what happens when we fail to share our light.

Today, we'll look at a well-known story to help us recognize spiritual selfishness. Many of us have heard the story of Jonah ever since we were children. A man gets eaten by a big fish and gets spit out after three days. What child wouldn't love that story? But the truth about Jonah is that he was selfish. He wanted to keep God's goodness and grace to himself and literally didn't want others to be saved. Let's look at this story in light of what we are talking about. Turn to the story of Jonah and read all four chapters before considering the following questions:

What was Jonah's heart toward the people of Nineveh?

What was God's heart for the people of Nineveh? (Hint: What does God say specifically about Nineveh in the last verse?)

The name Jonah means "dove."[17] A dove is often seen as a symbol of peace and compassion, yet when Jonah was asked to have compassion on the

Ninevites and bring them peace, he failed to live up to his name. In fact, not only did Jonah not want them saved—he was actually angry that they were saved. If you look again at Jonah 4:1–9, you will see Jonah's anger mentioned several times. Why does Jonah say he is angry in verse 4:2?

Now, to say that the Ninevites were evil is almost an understatement. The city of Nineveh was the capital of Assyria at that time, and the Assyrians were known for their horrific and gruesome treatment of those they captured. I won't go into all the gory details, but they were definitely a very wicked people. So when God asked Jonah to go to them preaching a message of repentance, it was for good reason that Jonah didn't want to go. It would be similar if you were asked to go preach repentance to the Nazis and Hitler during World War II. How would you feel about that? Would you be angry that God would want to offer such a group of people forgiveness? How about currently? Is there a person or group of people that you would run from if asked to go and offer them an opportunity to repent?

Thank God that He is not like you and me but is "merciful and gracious, slow to anger, and abounding in steadfast love and faithfulness." God is exceedingly patient and willing to forgive even the worst of sinners. And that is what God did here. He forgave the Ninevites when they repented. If it had been up to Jonah, the Ninevites wouldn't have had that opportunity to turn from their sin and repent.

What does 1 Timothy 2:3–4 further communicate about God's heart for people?

Now, look at a different Old Testament prophet, Isaiah. Read Isaiah 6:8–13, and then record Isaiah's response to God from Isaiah 6:8 below:

Such a dramatically different response than Jonah. How does Isaiah demonstrate God's heart?

Interestingly enough, God knew His people wouldn't respond or repent. Yet He still asked Isaiah to go, even though the response of the Israelites would be much different than that of the Ninevites. So you have two prophets: one refused to go, but the nation was later saved; one willingly went, but the nation wasn't saved. When you are sent, is the outcome up to you?

The truth is that we are responsible for our response, not the outcome. I know for me that relieves some pressure and anxiety. My responsibility is to respond in obedience to what God is calling me to do, not to do the work of the Holy Spirit in a person's life.

Timothy Pierce says, "If Jonah is about anything, it is about a God who reaches out to a world at total enmity with him and who asks his people to participate in that endeavor with him."[18] God is asking you to participate in reaching the world! Now, you may not be asked to save a whole people group, but He is asking you to have a willing heart toward wherever He asks you to go and with whomever He asks you to speak. He could be calling you to do youth ministry, help at a homeless shelter, visit a neighbor in need, become a foster parent, or even move to a foreign country. If He is, what will your response be? Will you run the other way, or will you jump up and say, "Here I am!"? Let's spend the rest of today in prayer. Ask the Lord to reveal any selfishness in your heart and ask where He would have you go or with whom He would have you speak.

Day 2

HIDING YOUR TALENTS

Today, we are going to look at the parable of the talents. A parable is a story that Jesus used to demonstrate a point or lesson, similar to a fable but without the animals. Go ahead and read through the parable in Matthew 25:14–30. As you read, identify what you think the moral of the story is. In fact, I want you to analyze this parable on your own first by answering the following questions, and then we'll look at it together.

Who are the main characters? List them below, and next to each character, record who you think he represents.

What is a talent, and what does it represent?

What do you think "he gave to each according to his own ability" means?

What did the first two servants do?

What did the third servant do?

When the master returned, how did he reward the first two servants?

How did he reward the third servant?

What was the reason the third servant gave for hiding his talent?

What do you think the moral of this parable is?

When we look at parables, it's important to notice the "whos" and "whys" because the people, things, and actions each represent something else. In this case, the master is Christ and the servants are His followers, or those who are believers. A talent in that time period was a measure of weight—not a specific coin but a measure of silver, gold, or a specific costly material. In verse 18, a "talent" is also referred to as money, so it was most likely a talent of silver. During Jesus's day, a denarius was a day's wages for the common worker, while a talent was worth six thousand denarii.[19] That's a huge sum of money! The amount is significant in that it highlights the Master's generosity. Whether it was one talent or five, those servants were given much more than they deserved.

It is essential to understand the significance of what these talents represented. They are often mistaken for the modern English meaning of "talent," a natural ability to do something, such as play the piano or soccer. However, I, as well as many other commentators, do not believe it is a literal talent Jesus is talking about. The talents in this Scripture signify degrees of faithfulness or responsibility. Christ gives us different portions of faith and accompanying responsibility. What is amazing is that He gives based on our abilities, because only He knows what we can handle and what we are capable of.

But even as He gives us according to what He knows we can do, we are still responsible for the doing. He doesn't force us to do what He knows we can. He gives us the opportunities to act. The first two servants acted immediately in order to double their master's money, while the third servant "dug" and "hid."

What do you think the *real* reason was that the servant did this?

Whatever the reason for his selfishness, the servant suffered the consequences for his lack of action. Jesus took his "talent" away, or, in other words, he took his responsibility away and gave it to someone else.

Do you think this is fair of Jesus? Why or why not?

Was this "money" theirs or the master's?

From our perspective, it may not seem fair, but Jesus has all the right to give and take away. Remember whom the "money" belonged to. The master was just asking the servants to be stewards with what was his.

Read Jeremiah 18:1–11. What did Jeremiah witness the potter doing?

How did this reflect what the Lord could do?

We may ask ourselves why, but the answer is right there: "it seemed good to the potter to do." Yet even as we're experiencing God's punishment, His care and grace are still seen. What does it say in verse 8 about "if the nation turns from evil"?

You see, Jesus loves you and wants His best for you. He wants us to participate in His work and obey what He is asking us to do. Even when He disciplines you or takes something away, He is waiting for you to repent and turn to Him. God knows the blessings, rewards, and joy that we will receive when we participate in His work. Remember the multiplication of the servants who did something with their talents? What was their reward? (Hint: There are three.)

The faithful servants were able to experience the increase with joy. Think of this as souls. Can you imagine the increase of people coming to salvation in the Lord Jesus Christ if you are responsible with what God has given you? Can you imagine hearing "Well done, good and faithful servant" when you get to heaven? Both thoughts thrill my soul!

One of my favorite lines in the Bible is from the second part of Luke 12:48. Write it down below:

This verse doesn't fill me with dread or burden me as a requirement. Instead, this verse encourages me and spurs me on. Sister, I've been given so much! You've been given so much! Regardless of what we physically have, we've been given salvation. We've been given life! That is a gift that we're meant not to just keep to ourselves but to share with others. The "talents" we've been given are meant to generate increase. We were blessed to be a blessing. What does this mean to you? Make a list of your "talents," describing what you've been blessed with and what the Lord has given you:

Let's conclude today with these questions: Are you hiding your "talents"? What kind of steward are you being with the faith, blessings, and responsibility that the Lord has given you?

Day 3

AS LONG AS IT DOESN'T HAPPEN TO ME

About a month ago, I was flying through Egypt. I was sitting next to a young Egyptian woman who had an infant and a toddler with her. I'm not kidding you, during the entire four-hour flight she took selfies. Ignoring her children's cries, oblivious to those around her, she just kept snapping away. In fact, for part of the flight, I held her children and comforted them as she continued to snap photos. Even though this is an extreme example, it seems to embody our culture. We live in a "selfie" culture. And though we may try hard not to become part of it, it does inevitably influence us. How often do we ignore the cries of others and what's happening around us because we are so focused on ourselves? For myself, it happens more often than I want to admit.

Let's look at the story of Hezekiah. Hezekiah was a king who walked in faithfulness and did what was right before the Lord. The Lord listened to his cries for help against the Assyrians and even granted him fifteen more years when he was sick and about to die. However, those last years seemed to have led Hezekiah into pride and selfishness. Read 2 Kings 20:12–19. (Also recorded in Isaiah 39:3–8.)

What did Hezekiah do with the men from Babylon?

Why would this be considered wrong?

What did Isaiah say would happen because of this?

What was Hezekiah's response?

Was the word of the Lord really "good"?

2 Chronicles tells us that "Hezekiah's heart was proud" (2 Chronicles 32:25). Unfortunately, often when we receive gifts from the Lord, we are tempted to believe it was by our own goodness and power, instead of by His grace. Yet even when given his punishment, Hezekiah remained proud. He was unwilling to admit his failure and didn't seem to care how the Lord's punishment would affect his people, even his own children. Some commentaries suggest that Hezekiah was merely accepting his punishment without complaint. However, prior to this, Hezekiah pleaded with the Lord, repented, and sought him (chapters 19 and 20). This time, instead of repenting and pleading with the Lord, he declared, "it was good." He considered the word of the Lord good because it was good for him, regardless of the fact that it was horrible for everyone else!

So how do we relate this to our own lives? We've been saved. We have forgiveness of sins and will someday live forever in the presence of God, where there is no more pain or suffering. However, what about the rest of the world? Will we be like Hezekiah and feel relief in that at least it won't happen to us?

Write down the following verses:

1 Corinthians 10:24

Philippians 2:3–4

What do these verses say about how we should act?

We often refer to selfishness in relation to the material things we have, like money, clothes, food, and other possessions. However, our greatest possession isn't material; it's our salvation. Look at 2 Corinthians 6:10 again: "as sorrowful, yet always rejoicing; as poor, yet making many rich; as having nothing, yet possessing everything." Whether we have material riches or not, we have spiritual riches. The gift of eternal life is our greatest possession, and it's one we can give away without actually giving it away. What I mean is that we can share this gift with someone without losing it ourselves. It's a case of multiplication, not subtraction. So, why don't we share it? Let's move beyond our own lives and care about what is going to happen to everyone else. Spend the last few minutes thanking God for the precious gift He's given you, and ask Him to help you not keep it to yourself.

Day 4

LEAVING THAT PLACE OF COMFORT

On the rare occasions that I get to visit a bookstore, I'm always surprised at the amount of self-help books. Authors, bloggers, and speakers are full of new information on how to make your life better, easier, and more comfortable. You see, the world's goal is ease and happiness. As believers, our goals should look very different, yet somehow that desire for ease and comfort slips into our lives. Even in our spiritual lives, we can seek ease and comfort. We can find ourselves looking for a church that makes us the most comfortable, we read books and Bible studies that only make us feel good, and we surround ourselves with like-minded friends. Not that any of these are in themselves wrong, but we may not even consider that God might be asking us to leave these places of comfort. Often, when faced with a difficult person, a difficult church, or a difficult circumstance, we look for a way out. For one reason or another, we believe that God would not want us in hardship, that hardship is not of the Lord.

Can you imagine if Jesus did this? If He refused to do the hard things and only did what satisfied Him and brought Him comfort? The salvation story would look a lot different! No sacrifice, no redemption of sins, no death on a cross. I'm so thankful that Jesus chose to give up what was easy and comfortable in order to save us. He gave up the easy in order that we may have life.

Jesus left His perfect heavenly home to come down to earth. Yet even on this earth, He didn't have a home. Read Matthew 8:19–20.

What did the young man want?

What was Jesus's reply?

Do you think Jesus was implying that the young man couldn't follow him or that he wouldn't want to follow him?

Much of the time, following Jesus means that we have to leave what is comfortable for something that is uncomfortable, unknown, and hard. Later in Matthew, Jesus told His disciples, "If anyone would come after me, let him deny himself and take up his cross and follow me. For whoever would save his life will lose it, but whoever loses his life for my sake will find it" (Matthew 16:24–25).

What do you think this looks like for you personally?

I'm not implying that you should look for the most difficult situation you can find and jump in, pack your bags and move to a foreign land, or sell everything you have and give it all to the poor. That is not what this is about. This is about obedience to whatever, wherever the Lord is calling you to—giving your life completely to Him and allowing Him to call you out of what is comfortable.

The reality is that comfortable places are not necessarily bad places; they are often good. Many times during His ministry, Jesus would escape to quiet places of solitude to pray to His Father in heaven. Oh, I can just imagine how peaceful and wonderful those intimate times with His Father must have been! But as much as He may have wanted to, Jesus didn't stay in those places of peace and rest. He continued to do the ministry that was before Him, even when it was hard.

Read the following verses. Recognize how Jesus took time away to pray, rest, and seek the will of His Father. Also note how He didn't stay in those places but continued to serve those around Him.

Matthew 14:13–14

Mark 1:35–38

Luke 5:15–16

Can you relate to this? Has there been a time (or times) when it has been hard to leave a good place to do what God has called you to do?

I often feel this way when I go on a retreat or even in my own daily quiet time. I don't want to leave that quiet, peaceful place and face "real life." Many mornings, as my kids are banging on the door yelling for this or that, and I'm facing the crazy amount of work I need to do and the many needs around me, I just want to stay in my comfortable chair with my coffee and my Bible. We can't neglect times of rest, rejuvenation, reading His Word, and listening to our Father in heaven. However, we have to fight the temptation to stay in those places—staying in those places that make us feel good, that don't cause stress, that keep us safe. Our challenge is to find the balance. As we are called to shine like Jesus, we can learn from His example. As He prayed and found times of solitude, let us find rest and times of solitude. And as He didn't neglect the work before Him and the mission He had to be a light, let us not stay hidden or neglect our mission. Let's continue in the work before us and leave those comfortable places when called.

Day 5

SERVING OUR MASTER

Dr. Gerald D. Robinson has a humorous, but very poignant, theology that he's titled Cat and Dog Theology. It addresses the trend of Christians using our Master mainly to get what we want: "A dog says, 'You pet me, you feed me, you shelter me, you love me, *You must be God*!' A cat says, 'You pet me, you feed me, you shelter me, you love me, *I must be God*!'"[20] You see, though they are given the same treatment, they have different perceptions of their master.

How do you look at God? Is He your Master whom you exist to serve, or your Master who exists to serve you?

____

____

As we've discussed the issue of not sharing our lights due to selfishness this week, we must now ask the question, How can we change this? Well, the opposite of selfishness is servanthood. We are to become servants. And in order to do this, we look at the life of the ultimate servant, Jesus Christ, who simultaneously is our one true Master.

Jesus was called "Master" many times in the Gospels, often when people were crying out to Him in need and desperation. One such occurrence was in Luke 8:24, when the disciples were caught in a storm. In fear for their lives, "they went and woke him, saying, 'Master, Master, we are perishing!'

And he awoke and rebuked the wind and raging waves, and they ceased, and there was calm." Another occurrence was in Luke 17:12–14, when ten lepers cried out, "Jesus, Master, have mercy on us," and were instantly healed.

In both these occurrences, how did Jesus display His authority?

Though Jesus had all authority, He treated it very differently than others treated their authority. Read Mark 10:42–45.

How does Jesus use His authority?

How does He tell us to behave?

Jesus demonstrated how we are to exercise authority by serving others. One of the most beautiful ways Jesus demonstrated this was when He washed His disciples' feet in John 13:1–17. Read that Scripture and then record what Jesus told His disciples to do in verses 14–17:

Can you think of examples of how you serve others? I know that those of us who are moms can easily give examples of ways we serve others. We serve all day long, changing diapers, doing laundry, cleaning the house, making food—the list goes on and on. In fact, I think we can get so drained from our daily acts of service that we do two things: first, we neglect to serve those outside our home, and second, we serve out of a grumbling heart.

I know you are probably all too familiar with the Proverbs 31 woman. Sometimes I hate that woman, don't you? Just kidding! But she does seem larger than life and an impossible example to follow. However, it's not about all the things that she does but her heart behind her actions. There are sweet truths we can learn from her. Can you please read Proverbs 31:10–31 and answer the following questions?

In what ways does she provide for her household?

____

____

In what ways does this woman serve others outside her household?

____

____

What do you think the last line, "let her works praise her," means?

____

____

Even with all that she does for her household, she doesn't neglect those outside her home. Her acts of service go beyond her doorstep. I'm sure these acts influenced her children as they observed her serving those outside her home and as they were taught to serve alongside her. You see, our children follow by example, so as we serve, they are taught to serve.

However, as we serve, whether in our home or outside, let's make sure we do it with the right heart. Record Philippians 2:14–15 below:

____

____

____

____

Whether you are a mom or not, this applies to us all. In order to shine as lights in the world, we need to serve without grumbling or disputing.

Easier said than done, I know! But I truly believe it comes down to our hearts and motivation. What is your motivation in serving?

The apostle Paul exhibits another great example of a servant. He states his motivation in Acts 20:24. Paul says, "But I do not account my life of any value nor as precious to myself, if only I may finish my course and the ministry that I received from the Lord Jesus, to testify to the gospel of the grace of God." Paul's motivation was the gospel. He was willing to give up his own needs and wants for the sake of the ministry of Jesus Christ. What we are being called to is not easy—to empty ourselves, not value our lives, count others as more significant than ourselves. Yet it's for the sake of the gospel, that others would come to know Jesus, that we serve and put others first.

I need to pause here, though, and make a quick point. We could also take this to an extreme and neglect ourselves in a way that is harmful. I've seen firsthand those who undermine their own needs and in the process hurt not only themselves but the people around them. That is not biblical, either. There is a balance between seeing yourself as precious and loved by God, thus caring for yourself, and giving up your life to love others and love God. What do you see as the balance? How do you serve others but also take care of yourself?

There is one more verse from Paul that I want you to look at before we close. 1 Corinthians 9:19 says, "For though I am free from all, I have made myself a servant to all, that I might win more of them."

What do you think "might win more of them" means?

Let's apply this to our own lives. We are free—free from sin, death, and eternal separation from God. How might we use that freedom to be servants so that we may "win more of them"?

Let's return to Dr. Gerald D. Robinson. He has this beautiful saying called "joyful conviction." Joyful conviction is when your heart is open to the Spirit prompting you to change. Were you joyfully convicted of any selfishness in your faith this week? If so, share it below. Spend time with your Master, asking Him how you can serve others and shine for Him in a greater way.

Week 6:
The Dim Light

Day 1

BECOMING WEARY

We've discussed hiding our light, whether from fear or selfishness, but sometimes, our light just grows dim. Our passion, love, and faith seem to ebb away, just as a flashlight slowly dims as the battery dies. What causes this dimness, and what can we do about it?

The Scripture calls this being lukewarm—you are neither hot nor cold. Look at Revelation 3:15–16. What does God say He will do with those who are lukewarm?

....

....

Yikes! Does this revelation put fear in your heart? God would rather you be hot or cold than be somewhere in the middle. I liken the term lukewarm to being dim, because a dim light emits an insufficient amount of light. Having a dim light usually goes hand in hand with apathy. The definition of "apathy," according to *Merriam-Webster*, is "a lack of feeling or emotion; lack of interest or concern."[21] If you are dim, you've lost the desire or concern for others and for God. Apathy comes in many shapes and sizes and for various reasons. We may be burnt out, we might be in a place of waiting that seems to go on and on, we may be distracted, or we may just find that we've lost our initial desire and love for God.

Do you ever feel like this? If so, what do you think is the cause?

This week, we'll discuss a few reasons why our lights grow dim. The first reason I see, and have experienced myself, is that we become weary. We often refer to this as being "burnt out." We use this term when we've worked too hard, overextended ourselves, or tried to create change with little result. We feel like we're fighting a losing battle, so we grow discouraged and tired. We stop caring or putting time into whatever we were working toward, and we close ourselves off. This goes beyond taking breaks or needing times of solitude and rejuvenation—we feel completely spent and done. I think most people, especially when it comes to ministry, feel this way at one point or another. Even the prophet Isaiah felt this. Look at Isaiah 49:4–5.

Why does Isaiah feel that his work is useless?

Despite feeling this way, what does Isaiah say?

Isaiah had it tough. I mean, he was desperately trying to get the Israelites to repent and turn from their sin. And in the long run, they still didn't listen to him. So, understandably, Isaiah felt that he had labored in vain. His work felt useless. Yet, even though he felt this way, he was able to give his work to the Lord and trust the Lord to do the work. He allowed the Lord to work through him to "be a light to the gentiles and bring salvation to the ends of the earth (Isaiah 49:6)."

Now turn to the New Testament. Record Galatians 6:9–10:

What does it mean that in "due season we will reap"?

Have you grown weary in doing good? How so?

Also look at Hebrews 12:1–3. What do we need to cast aside and consider in order to run the race with endurance?

Is there something specific in your life that you need to cast aside?

One specific thing that I believe most of us struggle with and need to cast aside in order to avoid growing weary is expectations. Expectations lead us to strive for results that are sometimes unattainable. And usually it is not God who puts the expectations on us, but ourselves and the world.

What are the world's expectations of you? What expectations do you hold for yourself?

What do you think God's expectations are for you?

Jesus tells us in Matthew 11:28–30, "Come to me, all you who labor and are heavy laden, and I will give you rest. Take my yoke upon you, and learn from me, for I am gentle and lowly in heart, and you will find rest for your souls. For my yoke is easy, and my burden is light." What does this mean to you?

The burden that is heavy is the world's! His burden is light because He carries us! Why do I say He carries us? Record these verses below:

Deuteronomy 1:30–31

Isaiah 40:11

How do these verses make you feel? I hope they fill you with the assurance that the Lord loves you. He wants to carry your burdens and give you rest. So, in light of what we've discussed today, how can you move forward after becoming burnt out or encourage someone you know who feels like this?

Day 2

WAITING

There is another type of weariness that comes through waiting. Every person on this earth has times of waiting: waiting for the right person to marry, waiting for a job, waiting for a child, waiting for a breakthrough. At any given time we are waiting for something. In fact, what are you waiting for right now?

During these seasons of waiting, we can become frustrated, disillusioned, and ultimately apathetic. We can start to doubt the Lord's promises and that He has our good in mind. Our faith and light can so easily dim during these trying times. Let's start by looking at a few biblical examples of people who had to wait.

Read Genesis 12:1–7 for the promise and Genesis 21:1–7 for the fulfillment.

What were Abraham and Sarah waiting for?

How long did they have to wait? (Hint: Note ages in 12:4 and 21:5)

Next, look at Genesis 29:15–28.

What was Jacob waiting for?

How long did he wait?

Let's also look at two New Testament characters, Simeon and Anna. Read Luke 2:25–38.

What were these two people waiting for?

How long did they wait?

Like these valiant men and women of old, we will find ourselves in times of waiting. Though it may seem that we are waiting on the actual things—children, marriage, jobs, freedom, etc.—the reality is that we are waiting on the Lord. It is the Lord who may allow these things to happen in His perfect time.

No one says waiting is easy. Joseph had an extremely difficult thirteen years before his dreams were fulfilled. During his "wait," Joseph was sold as a slave, falsely accused, and thrown into jail. Times of waiting are challenging. That is why Scripture tells us, "Be strong, and let your heart take courage, all you who wait for the Lord!" (Psalm 31:24)

Turn a little further in your Bible, to Psalm 37:7–9. Answer the following questions:

What are we to do while waiting?

Why, do you think, would it be easy to get angry while waiting?

What is God's promise for those who wait (verse 9)?

Also look at James 5:7–8. How are we to wait as a farmer does?

I want you to think about how a farmer waits for the fruit of his harvest. A farmer continually cultivates the ground. He doesn't stop his work just because he is waiting. We also can't stop our work just because we are waiting. I think our natural instinct is to stop everything else when we are in a season of waiting. We may not feel like doing ministry, meeting people's needs, or pursuing other things, because we just want that one thing so much. The problem is that as we just sit and wait, our light could easily grow dim, and the ground God has given us will remain stagnant and unfertile.

Another mistake we must avoid when waiting is doing the opposite of nothing and forcing something to happen. We often call this "making an Ishmael." You see, Ishmael was born because Abraham got tired of waiting and took matters into his own hands. Read Genesis 16:1–15.

What resulted from Sarai and Abraham taking matters into their own hands?

Yet, even though Abraham tried to do things on his own, he still retained the promise of God. Hebrews 6:15 tells us, "And thus Abraham, having patiently waited, obtained the promise." A few verses earlier in Hebrews, we are encouraged to imitate those men and women of faith such as Abraham. Please record Hebrews 6:11–12 below:

The ESV uses the word "sluggish." What prevents us from becoming sluggish?

Remember, it is impossible for God to lie, so when He makes a promise, you can believe that promise will come true. Will it always be in the timing you want it to be? No. Will it always be in the way you thought it would be? No. But we "have this sure and steadfast anchor of the soul" (Hebrews 6:19) that Jesus is our hope, and everything that He wants accomplished will be. We may think God is slow in fulfilling His promises, but it's for our own benefit that He waits. What does 2 Peter 3:9 say about this?

Later, in verse 15, Peter says, "and count the patience of the Lord as salvation." The Lord is waiting too! He is waiting for that day when He will judge the world, when all things will be made new and the powers of darkness will be overthrown for good. The Lord's infinite patience is what is allowing us the time to receive salvation and share it with others. Thank God that He waited for us! Thank God that we can wait, knowing His timing is perfect!

Day 3

LURE OF WEALTH

My husband is very passionate about farming. He calls it a hobby. I call it an obsession. He enjoys trying new farming techniques, and his "experiments" have taken over our yard. Yet the reality of farming is that it is precarious work. There are many elements that can harm your crop—disease, lack of rain, too much rain, weeds, insects, etc. Jesus knew these truths as He gave us the following parable.

The parable of the sower is found in Matthew, Mark, and Luke. Let's read it in Matthew 13:3–23. In this parable, the sower plants seeds that produce four different outcomes. Jesus then goes on to explain what these outcomes represent.

What does the seed represent?

Record what each outcome represents according to God's Word:

1. Seed fell by the wayside, and the birds ate it:

2. Seed fell on stony ground, so the roots did not go down deep and the plants withered in the hot sun:

____

____

3. Seed fell among thorns, and the thorns choked out the plants:

____

____

4. Seed fell on good ground and yielded a crop of multiple amounts:

____

____

Jesus is giving us a warning of what could happen to the Word of God in these situations. Let's focus on the third situation—the seed that fell among thorns and was choked out. Using your answer from above, why do you think riches and cares of this world "choke" our faith?

____

____

There is no one reason why our lights dim or why our faith, once vibrant and strong, is now stagnant and dull. However, as we look at Scriptures such as this one, we can see how the lure of wealth can cause our light to dim or even be snuffed out.

At the beginning of this week, we looked at Revelation 3:15–16, which warns us from being lukewarm. Revelation 3:17 continues on to say, "For you say, I am rich, I have prospered, and I need nothing, not realizing that you are wretched, pitiable, poor, blind, and naked."

Remember when we discussed that the goal of darkness is to blind us? Well, wealth is another tool used to blind us. The devil uses it to lure us into thinking we don't need God and that our resources, our hard work, and our prosperity can provide all that we need. This isn't to suggest that if you are wealthy, you are not a believer and don't have faith. By no means can we make that kind of judgment. In fact, there are many Scripture passages that identify people of wealth who further the kingdom and demonstrate tremendous faith. Some of those examples are King Solomon, Zacchaeus, and the centurion who asked Jesus to heal his servant. Let's take a few moments to look at the centurion.

Look at Luke 7:1–10.

What reveals this man was "rich"?

____

____

What kind of character did this centurion demonstrate?

____

____

What did Jesus say about him?

____

____

Faith is not determined by our wealth. In fact, the reality is that wealth is a moving target. What is wealth to you? Record a monthly salary that you would consider wealthy:

____

My husband asked a group of Ugandan pastors the same question. Some said the equivalent of $5 a day, some $10—one even said $50 a day. Consider the largest amount, $50 a day, which totals $1,500 a month: is that wealthy to you? It's all about perspective. So honestly, having money isn't the problem. The problem has to do with the heart and how we *rely* on money. It's also an issue of how we spend the money that we have and the responsibility we have with what God has given us.

1 Timothy 6:17–19 speaks to the rich. Read it and fill in the chart below.

What are the rich to do?	What are the rich not to do?

How do you think living this way would cause our lights to shine?

I truly believe that if we live this way, our lights would not grow dim or be choked out but would shine forth through our good deeds and love. What we do with our money and how we view money are very important aspects of being lights. Let's not let this tangible, fleeting object choke out our light.

Day 4

IN THE WORLD, NOT OF THE WORLD

There's not much use to lighting a candle in a well-lit room. You might enjoy the fragrance and a dim light, but the candle's usefulness is diminished in the light of the room. Now, please don't take me the wrong way, but our usefulness as lights is diminished when we only stay in places of light. We actually need to be in the dark in order to shine. In other words, we need to live in the "world" if we are to be lights. I'm sure you've heard the slogan "In the world, not of the world." This saying is taken from John 17. Let's look at it.

I want you to read John 17 in its entirety, because this prayer is beautiful as a whole. Though we know Jesus prayed a lot, this is one of the only recorded prayers, and He prayed it for us! It was a prayer for His disciples and for those who follow after them, which means that it is for you and me! It is such a rich, encouraging text for us as believers. Once you've read it, focus on verses 16 and 18, and record them below.

What does it mean to you to not be of the world?

Jesus says, "I have sent them into the world." List the ways you have been sent into the world:

If you can't think of many ways you have been sent, look around you. Do you have neighbors who aren't saved? What about coworkers? Do you have extended family members or friends who aren't believers? This is your world! The amazing thing is that your world will look different from mine. No two people have the exact same circle of friends, neighbors, coworkers, and family. We each have unique opportunities to share God's love and be His light with the people He put around us. Twice in this prayer Jesus states, "so that the world may believe that You sent Me." Do you recall what the ultimate goal of light is? We, as Jesus's disciples, are to be in the world so that the world may believe in Jesus Christ.

Sometimes, however, we have to fight the urge to stay in our "Christian bubbles." We've already discussed how fear and selfishness keep us from shining as the Lord has commanded us. The reality is, our lights aren't reaching their full potential in only bright environments. Our lights are dimmed when we neglect the dark world we were sent to.

I'm not saying don't hang out with those who are in the light. You must also surround yourself with believers that will edify you, encourage you, feed you the Word of God, and challenge you. This is necessary. 1 John 1:7 says, "But if we walk in the light as He is in the light, we have fellowship with one another, and the blood of Jesus Christ His Son cleanses us from all sin." What does having fellowship with one another look like?

Also take a look at Hebrews 10:24–25. What does it say we are not to forsake/neglect?

Can you see the balance of spending time with both believers and nonbelievers? I think of it like this: I spend time at church, at Bible studies, and with my Christian friends so that my light can grow brighter and stronger, but then I take my light into the dark places that the Lord shows me. I take my light to my neighbor, to the mall, to the slums, or even overseas to the people and places God calls me. But wherever God has called me, I can't neglect the fellowship of believers.

Spend the rest of today's lesson thinking of the ways you are being sent into the world. Ask the Lord who He would have you speak with and spend time with, where He wants you to go, and ways He wants you to get out of the well-lit areas of your life. You can record your thoughts and prayers below. I pray the Lord would reveal His will for you to be His light and that you would respond to His prompting.

Day 5

RETURN TO YOUR FIRST LOVE

This week, we've discussed how our lights can go from strong and vibrant to dim and flickering. Today, we'll look at one more cause: losing our first love. Sadly, this has happened to me, and though I hope it's never happened to you, I know many people who struggle with this feeling. The fire dims, the passion dies, the love we first had is just not the same. We are like the church of Ephesus in Revelation. Let's look at Scripture to see what God says about this when it happens and what we should do.

Record Revelation 2:4–5 below:

____

____

____

____

What is this first love referring to?

____

____

Most commentators agree that this first love is referring to the church's initial love for God; that their once vibrant and passionate love for God has faded to a dull flickering flame. A few other commentators consider this love to be for one another and say that Christ is addressing the church's diminished love for their fellow man. I tend to agree with the first group of commentators—I believe that this Scripture is about our love for God. However, just as we've read in 1 John 4:20, you can't love God without loving others, so the two are very much intertwined. Both objects of love can be considered here, though our focus today will be on our love for God.

If we are in this position and have abandoned our first love, we are told do three things. What are they?

1) ____________________

2) ____________________

3) ____________________

Let's look at each of these actions. First, we must *remember*. When the joy we had when we were first saved has faded, we have to go back and remember what it was like when we first came to salvation—that moment when our hearts were wooed by the incredible love of Jesus, and we stepped from death into life. We need to remember how it was before we were saved, how Christ has forgiven us, and how much He has done in our lives.

Unfortunately, over time our memory fades, and we don't recognize the amazing life we now have in Christ Jesus. We also don't like to think about our past sin, so we purposefully forget what it was like before we were in Christ. This isn't to say that the Lord remembers our sin or holds it over us. He doesn't! Look at the following two verses and write down what they say about God remembering our sins:

Isaiah 43:25

____

____

Hebrews 10:12–17

____

____

However, there is value in remembering our lives before salvation. How can we recognize all that God has done for us without first remembering from where He has brought us, and from what He has delivered us? In fact, God demands us to remember. Read Deuteronomy 8:1–20.

What does God warn the people of?

____

____

Why do blessing and abundance cause us, like the Israelites, to forget?

____

____

1 Chronicles 16:12 says, "Remember the wondrous works that he has done, his miracles and the judgments he uttered." So let's remember! Deuteronomy 8:14–15 is written below, but I've taken out what God did for Israel. Replace what God did for Israel with what He has done for you. Remember all the marvelous things God has done for you!

Do not become proud at that time and forget the Lord your God, who

____

____

Do not forget that He ______________________________

He gave you ____________________________________

Of course, we could fill hundreds of pages with all that the Lord has done, but by starting with a few, we recognize God's goodness in our lives and *remember* Him. And this remembering inevitably fans those diminished flames of love, which leads to the second action, to *repent*. To repent is to confess our sins and turn from them. The sin Revelation 2 instructs us to repent from is not any general sin but specifically the sin of not loving God like we should. It is our lack of love we are confessing—the fact that we've forgotten how much Christ has done for us and that we have taken His work on the cross for granted. If you feel like you need to confess right now, take a few moments to do that. You can record your thoughts, prayers, or confession below if you'd like.

____

____

____

The third and final thing we must do is *the first works*. What are the first works? Well, works of love, of course!

I remember when I first fell in love with my husband. I couldn't get enough of him. I was constantly thinking about him, talking about him, doing nice things for him. In fact, the bags under my eyes testified to my efforts to spend every spare minute with him. Even though my love for my husband may not look as passionate after fifteen years, those feelings are just as vibrant and strong. As you remembered that first encounter with God and how you fell in love with Him, did that stir in you a longing for those moments of first love? Did you long for those times when you were so passionately in love with Him that you would do anything to spend time in His presence, that you told everyone you met about His love, and that you willingly obeyed His commandments? If that is you, I urge you to return to that first love. Light that fire again!

Romans 12:11–13 says, "Do not be slothful in zeal, be fervent in spirit, serve the Lord. Rejoice in hope, be patient in tribulation, be constant in prayer. Contribute to the needs of the saints and seek to show hospitality." The definition of fervent is "very hot or glowing."[22] Consider the Scripture we read through this week. How do we keep that fire in our hearts red-hot or glowing?

If you are in one of these seasons of dimness we've discussed this week, I hope you are encouraged with this last thought: His love for you will never dim! As God says in Jeremiah 31:3, "I have loved you with an everlasting love; therefore I have continued my faithfulness to you."

Week 7:
From Candles to Beacons

Day 1

WAKE UP!

In the darkness and the storms, a lighthouse's beacon shines as a warning of death and destruction. Upon seeing the light, ships have the opportunity to change their course in order to avoid the rocky shallows that are ahead. Our light functions in the same way. As we light up the darkness, people have an opportunity to change their course to avoid the death and destruction ahead.

At this point, we may be ready to be lights but just aren't yet sure exactly how to do that. This week, we are going to look at specific ways in which we can shine. My desire is for us to go from being candles to being beacons of hope and life.

I find that many times I'm willing and wanting to shine, but I get distracted by life, and I'm not aware of what the Lord is asking me to do. This especially hit home one day at an American grocery store. I was standing at the checkout line, thinking about the day, the to-do list, my kids, and miscellaneous things. I wasn't aware of what was going on around me. After a few minutes, though, I realized that it was taking longer to check out than usual. I then noticed that the lady ahead of me was counting coins in order to pay for her items—and that her items were only the bare essentials. As she counted her pennies, it dawned on me that she didn't have enough money to pay for what she needed. I recognized that this was an opportunity to be a light and that the Lord wanted me to pay for her groceries. I quickly spoke up to say I would pay for her items along with mine. Now, I don't tell you that story to get accolades. The fact is, I was horrified. I was so close to missing an opportunity to be a light just because I was distracted. I didn't have my eyes open. In other words, I needed to wake up!

I wonder how many times I've done this. How many times have I missed an opportunity because I didn't have my eyes open? How about you? Can you give an example of a time this may have happened to you?

Today we are going to look at what the Bible says about "waking up" and being prepared so that we don't miss another opportunity to be God's light. The first Scripture that we will look at is the parable of the ten virgins in Matthew 25. Go ahead and read Matthew 25:1–13.

What was the difference between the wise virgins and the foolish virgins?

When the bridegroom was delayed, what did these young ladies do?

What do you think was the main point Jesus was trying to make with this parable?

In this parable the bridegroom represents Jesus and His return for us (the church). Just as the virgins did not know the hour of the bridegroom's arrival, we do not know the time that Jesus will return. "But concerning that day or hour no one knows, not even the angels of heaven, nor the

Son, but the Father only" (Matthew 24:36). It was the unpreparedness of the foolish virgins that prevented them from going with the bridegroom. They allowed their lights to go out, which left them in the dark.

My first instinct is to think that this wasn't fair. It wasn't fair for the five virgins to be left behind just because of a simple mistake. However, it wasn't just a simple mistake. The virgins in that time had an important role to play in illuminating the path of the bridegroom. Without light, the bridegroom would not be able to reach his bride. Their purpose as light bearers was essential to the wedding.

Do you believe that your role as light bearer is significant to Christ?

....

....

Not only did these virgins not take their roles seriously, but they were also lazy and unprepared. Alfred, Lord Tennyson wrote the following poem on this parable:

> Late, late so late! and dark the night and chill!
> Late, late so late! but we can enter still.
> "Too late, too late! ye cannot enter now."
>
> No light had we; for that we do repent;
> And learning this, the bridegroom will relent.
> "Too late, too late! ye cannot enter now."
>
> No light: so late! and dark and chill the night!
> O let us in, that we may find the light!
> "Too late, too late: ye cannot enter now."
>
> Have we not heard the bridegroom is so sweet?
> O let us in, tho' late, to kiss his feet!
> "No, no; too late! ye cannot enter now."[23]

What assumptions did the virgins make, according to this poem?

Honestly, this poem makes me a bit sad, but at the same time, it is super convicting. We can't waste time! We have to be prepared! William David Davies and Dale C. Allison Jr. summarize the point of this parable by saying, "They do not have enough time at this point because earlier they had too much time."[24]

Consider how you are using your time. Are there things you are putting off for later? Are you distracted by life to a point where you are missing opportunities?

Though these ladies may have run out of time, you, dear sister, have not. You still have time to wake up, rekindle your light, and walk in the good things the Lord has prepared for you. Luke 12:35 tells us, "stay dressed for action and keep your lamps burning." Let's continue to learn from Scripture about how we can do this.

Read Romans 13:11–14, and respond to the following questions:

What does it mean that "salvation is nearer to us now than when we first believed"?

What do you think is the armor of light we are to put on?

How are we not to behave?

____

____

I want you to recognize that this wake-up call isn't about waking up from unbelief—it's addressing those who already believe in the Lord Jesus Christ. 1 Thessalonians 5:6–8 is a very similar Scripture. It says, "So let us not sleep, as others do, but let us keep awake and be sober. For those who sleep, sleep at night, and those who get drunk, are drunk at night. But since we belong to the day, let us be sober, having put on the breastplate of faith and love, and for a helmet the hope of salvation."

What does it mean to you to not sleep but keep awake? How can we be spiritually asleep?

____

____

What do these verses say to put on?

____

____

The armor of light mentioned in Romans 13 and the armor mentioned in 1 Thessalonians 5 correspond to the armor of God presented in Ephesians 6:11–18. Read those verses and list the items we need to put on:

1) ____

2) ____

3) ____

4) ____

5) ____

How do you think having the armor on would allow us to shine more?

We must be prepared and ready for battle. Elijah prayed in 2 Kings 6:17, "O Lord, please open his eyes that he may see," and the Lord opened his servant's eyes to see the spiritual army around him. You see, there is a spiritual battle going on around us, but we need to be awake and have our eyes opened in order to see it. Remember, we are battling for souls, and that is no small thing. So let's take these last moments to pray that our eyes would be opened. Pray that we would see what is around us—both the spiritual battle around us and the tangible needs of the people around us—so that we can light the way for the coming of the Lord. Record any thoughts below:

Day 2

WORSHIP

Have you ever tried to start a fire without kindling? During my first attempts at starting a fire, I would get four or five big logs, pile them on top of each other, and light a match. Nothing would happen. I quickly learned that before the large logs went on, you needed smaller pieces of wood, paper, and other scraps to start the fire. Only when the fire was going at a decent rate could you then add the big logs.

Worship is the kindling to our fire. You can't to do the big things (the works) when you don't have a steady life of worship. It's as John Piper says: "When the flame of worship burns with the heat of God's true worth, the light of missions will shine to the darkest peoples on earth."[25]

As we spend time in God's presence, worshiping Him, exulting in His name, we find true joy and a desire to make Him known. Record Psalm 89:15–16 below:

....

....

....

....

The world offers you temporary happiness through fleeting experiences such as entertainment, vacations, or buying that one thing you really wanted. However, God's presence is not fleeting, and only He can provide true happiness. I love this quote from A. W. Tozer. He says, "Trying to be happy without a sense of God's presence is like trying to have a bright day without the sun."

Worship leads us into the Lord's presence as we acknowledge who God is and focus our thoughts and love on Him. Worship comes in many different forms—through song, dance, prayer, enjoying a beautiful sunset, drawing a picture, etc. You can be alone or with a body of believers. You can worship at church, on a hike, in your bathroom—anywhere.

How do you personally like to worship?

Next read Psalm 145:1–13 and answer the questions below:

What are some of the descriptions of God in these verses?

Write down all the verbs that we (the saints/the generation/His works) are to do in response of His greatness.

How does our worship work to "pour forth the fame of (His) abundant goodness"?

I love all the action in these verses. As we worship, we are naturally led to speak of God's greatness, sing of His righteousness, and make known His mighty deeds. The outpouring of worship is sharing Christ and what He has done for us with others.

What does this personally mean to you? List ways in which you can tell others about God's goodness, keeping worship in mind:

____

____

In this day and age with social media, we have so many opportunities to share God's goodness. It can be as easy as sharing what He did for you today on Facebook or putting a Scripture up on Instagram. But even beyond social media, you have daily opportunities to share as someone asks how you are doing, as you run into a stranger at the grocery store, or even as you speak into your children's lives. The more you practice worship, the more worship will infiltrate your entire day and will radiate out to everyone you come into contact with.

Please read 1 Peter 2:9.

You are . . . (List what you are as described in this verse.)

1) ________________________________

2) ________________________________

3) ________________________________

4) ________________________________

What beautiful truths that speak of our identity! And when we recognize our identity in Christ, we then have the motivation and desire to do what?

____

____

We have been called out of darkness into His glorious light! Our gratitude and praise pour out because of His wonderful works. Isaiah 63:7 says,

> I will recount the steadfast love of the Lord,
>
> the praises of the Lord,

according to all that the Lord has granted us,
and the great goodness to the house of Israel
that he has granted them according to his compassion,
according to the abundance of his steadfast love.

The steadfast love of the Lord has granted not only Israel good things, but you. Recount some of the good things the Lord has done for you in this last week or month, or even over the years.

Rejoice, dear sister, in who God is and in what He has done for you, and declare His amazing acts to the people around you. Let's end today in a time of worship. However you like to worship, spend the last minutes of your study time worshiping your Creator and Savior, Jesus Christ.

Day 3

OUR WORKS—PART 1

With worship kindling the fire, it is now time to add the larger logs: works. Our works display our worship. However, before we look at the specific works that the Lord has asked us to walk in so we shine, let's discuss the correlation between works and faith. Many people struggle with finding the balance of both, but balance is what we must find.

We've already read a portion of James 2, but now let's read James 2:14–26 more thoroughly.

Record verse 22 below:

____

____

What do you think happens if you have faith but not works?

____

____

What about vice versa? What if you have works but not faith?

____

____

How do faith and works work together?

____

____

Our works do not save us! Read the following verses, then record what all these verses are telling you:

Ephesians 2:8–9

Romans 11:6

2 Timothy 1:9

We are saved by faith, but our works reveal what we believe to be true. James uses Abraham as an example of someone who was justified by his works through faith. Abraham's faith was revealed by his actions of obedience to God. Can people see faith? No! But they sure can see the works of the faithful displaying God's goodness, His love, and His forgiveness.

Now look at these verses about our works and record what you find below:

1 Corinthians 3:13–15

Titus 1:16

James 1:22–27

From my perspective, we struggle with the pendulum swinging between works and faith. There will always be those who side on either extreme—faith without works, works without faith. The difficult part is living within the tension of the middle. Do you understand how that is possible, though?

I think of it like this: My husband could tell me he loves me every day, all day long, but without actions that follow suit, it would be really hard for me to believe him. I need him to show me his love by spending time with me, helping me around the house, and giving me lots of hugs and kisses. His actions prove his love. Our actions prove our love for God and for people.

When Jesus calls us to be lights to the world, He also calls us to good works. Go back and reread Matthew 5:14–15, but this time, include verse 16. How are our light and good works connected, according to this verse?

____

____

From this verse, what is the purpose of our good works?

____

____

Throughout this Bible study, we've mentioned many of the good works that we are to walk in so we shine. List a few of the good works that come to your mind that would allow our lights to shine:

____

____

God has asked you to partner with Him, to be His hands and feet in this dark world. We have the privilege of doing work that will bring Him glory and shine His light in the darkness. Please take a few moments to reflect on how your works are reflecting your faith. Ask God if your actions are revealing your faith to others. Are your works displaying your worship and love for God?

____

____

____

Day 4

OUR WORKS—PART 2

Please begin today by reading Ephesians 2:10 out loud: "For we are his workmanship, created in Christ Jesus for good works, which God prepared beforehand, that we should walk in them." Now read it out loud again, but this time, replace the "we" with "I."

You are His workmanship! Not only did God create you in such a beautiful, exceptional way; He is continuing to work on you and further mold you into His image. And His intent is for you to walk in the good works He has prepared for you. The God of the universe has prepared work for you! Does that make you feel special? It should! I'm reminded of the story of Esther when she was called upon to go before the king and plead for her people. Mordecai urged her forth with these words: "And who knows whether you have not come to the kingdom for such a time as this?" God has given you this time to rise up, to shine His light by the good works that He has prepared specifically for you.

So now you may ask, "what are the good works that I'm supposed to walk in?" Honestly, that is a very open-ended question, because the answer is unique to each of us. As you seek God, He will guide you with the Holy Spirit to move and do what He wants you to do. However, I do believe that the Scripture has given us some general guidelines of what needs are close to God's heart and what He would specifically like us to do.

We'll begin by looking at a few Old Testament passages that are addressed to the Israelites. Now, don't you go making the assumption that these commands were only for the Israelites. These commands are for all who follow God, as seen in how God gives these instructions for His initial people, the Israelites, but then continues to give the same instructions through His Son, Jesus, to all who follow Him—which means you and me. Open your Bible to the book of Isaiah and read Isaiah 58:1–10. Then answer the following questions.

According to this text, why would God be against a fast (a time of prayer in which you deny yourself food or other pleasures)?

....

....

List the actions God demands of you in order for "your light to break forth."

- ____
- ____
- ____
- ____

God demands action on behalf of others, not meaningless rituals for the sake of oneself. In fact, the act of fasting was only commanded by God twice in the Old Testament, yet there are hundreds of times He commanded justice, to take care of the needs of the poor, the stranger, and those who are oppressed.[26] God cares deeply about all of humanity, "your own flesh" so to speak, according to this text. He demands we respond to their needs, whether they be hunger, oppression, sickness, homelessness, or imprisonment. Your response is part of the "work" He has called you to in order that your light will shine forth.

Who do you consider to be the oppressed and afflicted?

God often refers to the orphan, the widow, the poor, and the stranger as those who are oppressed or afflicted because, sadly enough, it is those people who are the most vulnerable and get taken advantage of, abused, forgotten, and/or enslaved. God demands action, not lip service, as seen in the heavy consequences for those who disobey. In fact, you can see how Israel was punished for not obeying God in these areas. Read Zechariah 7:8–14.

What were the Israelites commanded to do?

What was the result of the Israelites' disobedience?

Again, you and I are not off the hook. Our obedience is also commanded when it comes to these specific works. Let's look at what Jesus had to say in the book of Matthew. We've already read the two previous parables in Matthew 25. Today we'll read Matthew 25:31–46, the finale of Jesus's recorded teachings before the Passover Supper and His death on the cross.

Who will be gathered, and how will they be separated?

What are the six works that Jesus used to judge?

1) ____________________

2) ____________________

3) ______________________________

4) ______________________________

5) ______________________________

6) ______________________________

Both groups were surprised at Jesus's judgment. What do you think was each group's reason for being surprised?

____

____

____

Again, we are discussing the final judgment. I hope you aren't tired of that topic yet, because its importance is critical to our ministry on this earth. There are a few points we need to notice from this parable. First, remember it is not by works that we are saved. This is confirmed in the fact that the righteous were actually surprised. They did not assume that because they did these good acts they would get into heaven. In fact, they were not even aware that "their little actions to the little people to whom they gave little thought were a big deal to Jesus."[27] It's the unassuming acts done in love that reveal we belong to Christ.

The second point is that when Jesus refers to "the least of these my brothers," He is most likely referring to His followers, though there are many commentators who believe that "the least" represents all who are in need. We've discussed this point before, as we've talked about love. Though it may start with our fellow brothers and sisters in Christ, it then extends to all people. However, I would agree that in this particular context, Jesus uses the word "brothers," which generally refers to Christians in the New Testament. I like how D. A. Carson put it. He said, "Good deeds done to Jesus' followers, even the least of them, are not only works of compassion and morality but reflect where people stand in relation to the kingdom and to Jesus himself. Jesus identifies himself with the fate of his followers and makes compassion for them equivalent to compassion for himself."[28]

Besides our "brother," God has also called us to love the stranger. Several times now we have read the word "stranger" or "sojourner." Who do you consider a "stranger"?

____

____

A stranger is a foreigner, someone who is not in their home environment, but that term can be used in many circumstances. It can be for a new neighbor, a refugee, or someone living outside the context of their culture. Here in Uganda, I am a stranger. I'm a minority within a different culture. But what I love and appreciate about this culture is how hospitable people are to the stranger. There is no call ahead. You can just stop by anyone's house, be invited in, and be offered water for washing and food to eat. They'll drop everything to accommodate a guest. I believe this culture has captured God's heart for the stranger.

The Israelites also knew what it was like to be a stranger. They were strangers in the land of Egypt before God rescued them and brought them to the Promised Land. And God continually reminded them of this as He gave them strict instructions to care for the strangers. Leviticus 19:33–34 says, "When a stranger sojourns with you in your land, you shall not do him wrong. You shall treat the stranger who sojourns with you as the native among you, and you shall love him as yourself, for you were strangers in the land of Egypt: I am the Lord your God."

What does Hebrews 13:1–2 further tell us about how we should treat strangers?

____

____

Wow! Isn't it pretty awe-inspiring that you could literally be entertaining angels when you invite a stranger in? This simple act of hospitality is a powerful way we can shine God's light. I want you to think of how you can apply this personally. Is there someone you've felt led to invite over for coffee or dinner? It doesn't have to be a complete stranger, but maybe just someone you would like to get to know—a neighbor, a colleague, a classmate, or a homeless person that you pass by every day. Do you have any refugees in your community that you could reach out to? Make a list of people you could invite, and start praying for the opportunity to have them over.

At this point you may be feeling overwhelmed by all the commands and tasks at hand, but let me encourage you: God is not calling you to "save the world." Jesus already did that. He is calling you to the simple tasks of love and will guide you in what those will be. Micah 6:8 says, "He has told you, O man, what is good; and what does the Lord require of you but to do justice, and to love kindness, and to walk humbly with your God?" It's as simple as that. Don't allow the "works" to become overwhelming or stressful, or to take the place of faith. Pray and allow the Spirit to guide you into the works that the Lord has prepared for you.

So let's end today doing that. Ask the Lord how you can help the poor, the stranger, the orphan, the widow, or anyone who is in need. How are you going to walk in obedience to these commands so that your light can shine forth like the dawn? Take the time to record your thoughts and what God is speaking to you below:

Day 5

WISDOM

When we *worship*, it will lead us to *work*, and through it all, we need *wisdom* to guide us in being a light. The last principle of shining brighter that we'll discuss is wisdom. In everything we do, we have to seek wisdom. Wisdom does not imply having an immense amount of knowledge or being book smart. It's knowing how to do the right thing with the knowledge that we do have. We've discussed wisdom a bit already, but we'll go into more detail today as we look at how crucial wisdom is to us shining brightly.

Let's begin by turning to the Old Testament and looking at the book of Daniel. Daniel was a literal "wise man." He served the Babylonian and Medo-Persian kings by giving them wise counsel. Though Daniel was exceedingly wise, he was well aware of where his wisdom came from. Read Daniel 2:17–23, which describes the time when King Nebuchadnezzar was about to kill all of the wise men because they couldn't tell him his dream.

How did Daniel seek wisdom?

____

____

Whom does Daniel recognize as the giver of wisdom and knowledge?

____

____

Daniel knew the same truth later indicated in James 1:5: "If any of you lacks wisdom, let him ask God, who gives generously to all without reproach, and it will be given him." He understood that it wasn't books, education, or other people that gave wisdom. It was the Lord! Daniel continued to receive visions and revelations from the Lord during his entire lifetime. In one such vision, the "angel" described some of the events that will happen during the end times. Look at what he says about those who are wise. Write down Daniel 12:3 below:

From this verse, what qualities should we have if we want to shine like the stars?

I find it interesting that wisdom and turning many to righteousness are qualities of those who shine like the stars. Proverbs 11:30 says, "The fruit of the righteous is a tree of life, and whoever captures souls is wise."

What does it mean to capture souls?

Aren't those beautiful words to picture, "to capture souls"? Remember, we discussed that a reason for being a light is to draw others to you in order to "capture" them with God's love. Now we read that those who capture souls and turn many to righteousness are considered wise. Would you consider yourself wise—maybe not in the scholarly academic sense, but in the sense that you seek God and seek to make Him known? That is the wisdom we want to strive for!

Another aspect of having wisdom is worship. You'll see that wisdom and worship are directly linked to one another. Read what Job 28:28 and Proverbs 9:10 say about wisdom.

What does the fear of the Lord mean to you?

As we worship God, we have the fear of the Lord because we recognize how powerful, how glorious, and how holy He is. He is the eternal judge, and His power no one can fathom, but He is also full of mercy, love, and grace for us. As we worship and recognize who God is, we will naturally grow in wisdom and understanding.

Wisdom is also a part of doing those good works we talked about this week. Read James 3:13–18.

What shows our wisdom?

Compare "false wisdom" with wisdom from above.

As we walk in wisdom, we'll know what to say to the stranger who asks, "Who is God?" We'll know what to do for that hurting child who looks so downcast at the playground. We'll know how to pray for the persecuted church in India. In everything, wisdom will guide us, and we'll be the light that we are meant to be. So, sister, I pray "that the God of our Lord Jesus Christ, the father of glory, may give you the Spirit of wisdom and of revelation in the knowledge of him" (Ephesians 1:17). I pray this so that we can shine as life-giving beacons through our wisdom, works, and worship.

Week 8:
For His Glory

Day 1

IT'S NOT OUR LIGHT

If you grew up going to church, you may remember the song "This Little Light of Mine." You would hold up your pointer finger, representing the candle, and sing, "This little light of mine, I'm gonna let it shine." Well, it would be more accurate if it said, "This little light of His, I'm gonna let it shine," because the reality is that it's not our light, it's His! He is the Light. He created the light, and it is He who shines through us.

As we conclude this study, we'll look again at the Giver of Light because the ultimate purpose of His light, the ultimate purpose of us being lights, is for His glory! Did you get that? Record this sentence below: My light is for God to be glorified!

....

....

In your own words, write down what this means to you:

....

....

Turn to 2 Corinthians 4:5–7 in order to answer the following questions.

From this Scripture, what is the "treasure" that is held in our perishable containers? (Hint: See verse 6.)

What reveals God's power to others?

God is the one who spoke light out of darkness, and only He has the power to overcome the blindness of this world. We are just the fragile jars of clay that contain this "treasure," the light of the gospel. There is significance in that we are likened to jars of clay. Look at the following Scriptures and record how you find they reveal we are like jars of clay:

Genesis 2:7

Job 10:9–12

Psalm 39:4–5

Isaiah 64:8

Why do you think it's important for us to understand the fragility, brevity, and origin of our lives?

____

____

In our weakness, He is strong. His power can be seen because it is not in our strength but His. So we can allow Him to use us as vessels of light for His glory and His sake.

Please write down 2 Corinthians 4:15:

____

____

What happens when grace extends to more and more people?

____

____

The reason I wrote this Bible study is so that God would receive more glory. You see, as more people are drawn to His light, as more people receive His salvation and grace, He is glorified! I look forward to and anticipate the day when "at the name of Jesus every knee should bow, in heaven and on earth and under the earth, and every tongue confess that Jesus Christ is Lord, to the glory of God the Father" (Philippians 2:10–11).

As we study God's glory this week, ponder what His glory actually means to you and how your light can glorify Him.

Day 2

HIS FACE WILL SHINE ON YOU

Let's start today by recording Numbers 6:24–26:

....

....

....

....

You've probably heard this prayer or blessing before if you've attended church for a while. Many churches close their services with these words. Can you believe we've carried on this tradition over thousands of years? The priests would say these words to the people after the morning sacrifice at the temple. In fact, God commanded the priests to say these words to the people. In Numbers 6:23 God says, "Speak to Aaron and his sons, saying, Thus you shall bless the people of Israel."

This same blessing could very well be the one that Jesus used right before He ascended in Luke 24:50. It says, "lifting up his hands he blessed them." Seeing as Jesus is our great High Priest, He would carry on the tradition of blessing the people in this way before He departed. So why is this blessing important to our study? First of all, it is a departing blessing, and as we conclude our study this week, it's a sweet Scripture of closure. But also, we need God's face to shine on us in order for us to reflect Him and to be lights ourselves. As we study God's glory this week, we ask for His glory to shine on us and try to understand how that is even possible.

"The Lord bless you and keep you."

"Bless you" is a common saying these days. We say "God bless you" when someone sneezes, "blessings" at the end of a letter, and "bless you" when someone does something kind. But what does "the Lord bless you" really mean? In your own words, what do these words mean to you?

The Lord's blessing is His favor upon you. "The Lord bless you" refers to the fact that He cares for you, loves you, and provides for you. God wants to bless you. In fact, from the very beginning, we can see God demonstrating His desire to bless (Genesis 1:22). Then, as He calls forth the Israelite people as His own, the same as He calls us as His own, He explains the blessing they will receive if they obey Him. Look at Deuteronomy 7:11–21.

What do these verses say God will do to bless His people?

What about keep you? The Hebrew word, *shamar*, used in this context, means to guard or to keep safe.[29] He is watching over you, keeping you safe, and guarding your life. Can you imagine that about your God? He keeps you and doesn't let you go.

In Genesis 28:15, the Lord says this to Jacob: "Behold, I am with you and will keep you wherever you go, and will bring you back to this land. For I will not leave you until I have done what I have promised to you." The same goes for us. God is with us. He keeps us wherever we go, under whatever circumstances—He will not leave us and will keep His promises.

"The LORD make his face to shine upon you and be gracious to you."

What do you think His face shining on you means?

The Lord's face and countenance are the same, so we'll discuss this below. First, let's look at what being gracious means. Look up the following verses on God's grace to understand how He is gracious to you.

Romans 3:21–24

Ephesians 1:7–10

How is God gracious to you?

"The LORD lift up his countenance upon you and give you peace."

When we ask for the Lord's countenance, again, we are referring to His face, both of which indicate His presence. Knowing God face-to-face is the greatest blessing there is. And not only do we have His presence, but we also have His love and approval. As God looks at us, He delights in us! Picture a loving father looking down on his children, his face radiating the joy and love he has for his children. That is how God looks at you.

Read Psalm 4:6–8. What does the light of the Lord's countenance give us, according to these verses?

How does this make you feel? Knowing that God looks at you in love, protects you, and gives you all that you need, does that fill you with peace?

The phrase "the Lord" is repeated three times, symbolizing the Trinity and emphasizing that He is the only one who gives blessing. We may seek blessing from others, from material possessions, or in our achievements, but God is the only one who blesses. And His blessing is not just for our benefit. Look at Psalm 67:1–2, which repeats the same blessing, but with something added:

> May God be gracious to us and bless us
>
> and make his face to shine upon us,
>
> that your way may be known on earth,
>
> your saving power among all nations.

What will result when God's face shines on us?

That's such a beautiful truth! As His face shines on us, not only are we blessed, but others are blessed. It is like God said to Moses in Genesis 12:2: "I will bless you and make your name great so that you will be a blessing." I love it! I pray that this will be such an encouragement to your soul today.

Day 3

REFLECTING HIS FACE

Yesterday, we talked about the Lord's face shining on us. Today, we'll discuss how we can amazingly reflect His face. I mean, it's incomprehensible that we can actually reflect God's glory. Think about His glory, His awesomeness, and His power actually being seen in us! That is what happens when we spend time in His presence.

Read Exodus 34:29–35.

Why did Moses's face shine?

....

....

How did the people react, and what did Moses do in response?

....

....

....

Just picture this! Moses was physically exuding light when he came down the mountain after being in the presence of God for forty days. The literal translation in Hebrew is "the skin of his face sent out horns," which leaves us with an odd picture of a horned Moses (actually depicted by medieval and Renaissance artists). However, that expression is in reality referring to rays of light, better pictured as radiant beams shining from his face.[30]

Just think: the remnant of glory that remained on Moses was just a miniscule fraction of God's actual glory. Yet even this small amount terrified the people as they recognized God's holiness and their sinfulness. They were so frightened that they asked Moses to cover his face.

Now read 2 Corinthians 3:12–18.

What (Who) takes away the veil?

How can we be transformed into His image and reflect His glory more?

Did you get that? All of us have the veil removed so that we can reflect the glory of God! We don't have to hide like Moses did because of people's fear. We can let it shine! And our brightness is "ever-increasing," as the NIV says, which means we are becoming more and more radiant as we become more like Christ.

Think about Moses. His face shone after He was in the presence of God. The more time we spend with God, the more we'll radiate Him. Spending time in God's presence can look many different ways. Name some ways we can practice being in the presence of God:

The moon is a powerful example of how we are to reflect God's glory. Remember back in Genesis 1:16 when God created the sun and moon? "And God made the two great lights—the greater light to rule the day and the lesser light to rule the night—and the stars." Interesting enough, the sun and stars all emit their own light. The moon does not. The moon shines because its hard, rocky surface reflects light from the sun. If you could look at the moon without the sun, it would appear just a dark, ugly rock. Yet, with the sun, it is a splendid light.

And when is the moon to preside? Yes, during the night. Just as the moon is to light up the darkness of night, so we are to light up the darkness. Yet how bright we shine depends on how we are turned to God. You see, another truth about the moon is that the reflection depends on its angle and rotation. Only the side of the moon facing the sun is lit by it; the rest is in darkness. Here, again, we see the truth that we have to be "facing God" if we are to reflect Him. Psalm 80:3 says, "Turn us again, O God, and cause thy face to shine; and we shall be saved" (KJV). Other versions say "restore us," but I like the visual picture of asking God to literally turn us to Him. Only when we are turned to Him can we reflect Him.

How can you relate the moon to your own life?

Now, record the following Scriptures below:

Colossians 3:9–10

Ephesians 4:21-24

According to these verses, how do we become renewed and become more like the image of God?

Something that I see in both of these Scriptures is that gaining knowledge is part of being renewed into the image of Christ. We need to be taught through the Scripture and the Spirit so we know how to truly reflect Christ. Again, this goes back to spending time in God's Word and in prayer. R. K. Hughes told the following story to further illustrate this:

> A man returning from a journey brought his wife a matchbox that would glow in the dark. After giving it to her she turned out the light, but the matchbox could not be seen. Both thought they had been cheated. Then the wife noticed some French words on the box and asked a friend to translate them. The inscription said, "If you want me to shine in the night, keep me in the light." We need to spend time alone with Jesus—the Light—in prayer, exposing our lives like photographic plates to His presence, so that his image, his character is burnt into ours.[31]

Today I want you to think about ways that you can turn to God in order to reflect Him. Thank Him that the veil has been removed and we can actually stand in the glory of His countenance. What an astounding privilege that is!

Day 4

THE GLORY OF THE LORD

I am completely inadequate to write this next lesson on the glory of the Lord. How can I, a feeble, sinful human being, begin to describe the glory of God? It is as Isaiah said when he saw the throne room of God in a vision, "Woe is me! For I am lost; for I am a man of unclean lips, and I dwell in the midst of a people of unclean lips" (Isaiah 6:5). We truly recognize our depravity when we catch a glimpse of how holy and glorious our Lord is. However, despite my inadequacy, the glory of the Lord is our second-to-last lesson, because His glory is the beginning and the end.

God's glory is the reason for this study, the reason we are alive, and the reason that we are lights. John Piper says this: "When the glory of God himself saturates our preaching and teaching and conversation and writings, and when he predominates above our talk of methods and strategies and psychological buzzwords and cultural trends, then the people might begin to feel that he is the central reality of their lives and that the spread of his glory is more important than all their possessions and all their plans."[32] Does God's glory saturate every part of your life? Is His glory your focus, your goal, and your reason for all that you do?

Today, let's bask in His presence like we discussed in the previous lesson. As you read through the following Scriptures depicting God's glory, note how each description contains a reference to light or a form of light. I also ask that you take your time today. Let His glory overwhelm your soul and captivate you. You'll notice that there is a lack of commentary today, because today is just about you and God. Sit at His feet and be in awe!

Record Exodus 24:16–17.

What is the glory of the Lord compared to?

Now turn a few chapters later to read what happens when Moses asks to see God's glory. This was right before Moses returned down the mountain with his face radiating the glory of the Lord, as we discussed in day 3. Read Exodus 33:18–34:8.

What truths does God proclaim about Himself?

What was Moses's response?

Next, read all of Psalm 104.

How is the Lord clothed in the first two verses?

What other aspects of God's glory stand out to you?

Ezekiel was granted a glimpse into the heavens and saw a vision of God. Read the description of this vision in Ezekiel 1.

How did the glory of the Lord appear to Ezekiel?

What was Ezekiel's response?

Finally, read Revelation 1:12–18.

How is Jesus described in these verses?

How did John react to what he saw?

How do these descriptions of God/Jesus make you feel?

What can I say that these Scriptures don't say themselves? I find it so easy to forget how glorious and powerful our God truly is. Yet when I read these Scriptures, I'm left speechless and fall to my knees in worship like those who recorded them. In fact, the Hebrew word for worship is *shachah*, which means to bow down or to fall down flat. That is the response of those who behold God's glory. I pray these Scriptures lead you to fall flat on your face in worship of the awesomeness of our Lord. Our God is worthy of all of our love, all of our life, and everything we have. As we shine, let's do so for His glory and never forget whom we serve!

Day 5

YOU ARE THE LIGHT OF THE WORLD!

Tears fill my eyes as we end this study. I love you, dear sister! I'm so thankful that you've taken this journey with me and have spent this time in God's Word. I pray that you feel challenged, encouraged, and most of all, more in love with God than you did before. He loves you with an incredible, all-sacrificing love! You are His child! And He wants you to light up His world! Will you do that? As we end today, I want you to reflect on this study. We've gone over a lot during the last two months, so the teacher in me recognizes the importance of reviewing as we conclude.

From week 1, what are our sources of light?

____

____

From week 2, what is the goal of darkness, and how does darkness accomplish this?

____

____

____

From week 3, what are the purposes of light?

From week 4, why do we hide our light, and how can we conquer that?

From week 5, what is spiritual selfishness, and what can we do about it?

From week 6, what are the leading causes of having a dim light?

From week 7, what are some specific ways in which we can shine brighter?

From week 8, what is the ultimate purpose of our light, and how can we accomplish this?

Are there any specific verses that spoke to you during this study?

I also want you to take some time to reflect on what the Lord may have challenged you with during this study. Has there been something that the Lord has asked you to do during the last eight weeks? Spend a sweet time of prayer and fellowship with your Lord and Savior today as you reflect on what He wants you to do. Ask Him how can you specifically light up your neighborhood, your city, and the world.

I pray that the Lord took out any words that weren't of Him and thoughts that were contrary to His Word and has just left His truths. May the Lord bless you and keep you. May He cause His face to shine on you! Go forward and shine, dear sister!

ENDNOTES

[1] Calvin, quoted in Ronald Youngblood, *The Book of Genesis* (Oregon: Wipf and Stock Publishers, 1991), 23.

[2] Alfred Edersheim, *Sketches of Jewish Social Life in the Days of Christ* (Grand Rapids, MI: Eerdmans, 1964), 268.

[3] R. K. Hughes, *John: That You May Believe* (Wheaton, IL: Crossway Books, 1999), 225.

[4] C. S. Lewis, *The Great Divorce* (London: The Centenary Press, 1945), 103.

[5] Leon Morris, *Tyndale New Testament Commentaries*, vol. 3, *Luke* (InterVarsity Press, 1988), 347.

[6] Calvin, quoted in Philip Edgcumbe Hughes, *Paul's Second Epistle to the Corinthians* (Eerdmans, 1962), 125.

[7] *Oxford Dictionary of English*, 3rd ed. (2010), s.v. "pride."

[8] C. S. Lewis, *Mere Christianity* (New York: Macmillan Publishing Company, 1952), 109.

[9] Joseph Parker, *The People's Bible*, vol. 27, *Ephesians–Revelation* (Grand Rapids, MI: Baker, 1959), 350.

[10] *Oxford Dictionary of English*, 3rd ed. (2010), s.v. "similitude."

[11] R. K. Hughes, *Ephesians: The Mystery of the Body of Christ* (Wheaton, IL: Crossway Books, 1990), 165.

[12] Klyne Snodgrass, *The NIV Application Commentary: Ephesians* (Zondervan, 1996), 273.

[13] Martin Luther, *The Catholic Epistles*, ed. Jaroslav Pelikan, vol. 30 of *Luther's Works*, (Concordia: Saint Lois, 1967), 301.

[14] Charles Spurgeon, *Treasury*, 569, quoted in D. L. Allen, *1–3 John: Fellowship in God's Family* (Wheaton, IL: Crossway, 2013), 206.

[15] Leon Morris, *Testaments of Love* (Grand Rapids, MI: Eerdmans Publishing, 1980), 221.

[16] *Merriam-Webster's Deluxe Dictionary* (Tenth Collegiate Edition, 1998), s.v. "selfish."

[17] James Bruckner, *The NIV Application Commentary: Jonah, Nahum, Habakkuk, Zephaniah* (Grand Rapids, MI: Zondervan, 2004), 41.

[18] Timothy Pierce, *Discovering the Mission of God Supplement* (Downers Grove, IL: InterVarsity Press, 2012), 216, e-book.

[19] Douglas Sean O'Donnell, *Matthew: All Authority in Heaven and on Earth* (Wheaton, IL: Crossway, 2013), 739.

[20] Gerald Robison and Bob Sjogren, *Cat and Dog Theology* (Downers Grove, IL: InterVarsity Press, 2005), 5. Emphasis added.

[21] *Merriam-Webster's Deluxe Dictionary* (Tenth Collegiate Edition, 1998), s.v. "apathy."

[22] *Merriam-Webster's Deluxe Dictionary* (Tenth Collegiate Edition, 1998). s.v. "fervent."

[23] Tennyson, quoted in Philip Schaff, *Christ in Song: Hymns of Immanuel Selected from All Ages* (Vestavia Hills, AL: Solid Ground Christian Books, repr. 2003), 307.

[24] W. D. Davies and Dale C. Allison Jr., *A Critical and Exegetical Commentary on the Gospel According to Saint Matthew*, vol. 3, 98, quoted in O'Donnell, *Matthew: All Authority in Heaven and on Earth* (Wheaton, IL: Crossway Books, 2013), 274.

[25] John Piper, *Let the Nations Be Glad* (Grand Rapids, MI: Baker Academic, 2003), 18.

[26] John N. Oswalt, *The NIV Application Commentary: Isaiah* (Grand Rapids, MI: Zondervan Publishing House, 2003), 625.

[27] Douglas Sean O'Donnell, *Matthew: All Authority in Heaven and on Earth* (Wheaton, IL: Crossway Books, 2013), 752.

[28] D. A. Carson, "Matthew," in *The Expositor's Bible Commentary*, vol. 9, rev. ed. (Grand Rapids, MI: Zondervan, 2010), p. 583. On pp. 583, 584 Carson lists scholarly studies that side with his position. Cf. Blomberg, *Preaching the Parables*, p. 213, n. 6.

[29] R. L. Thomas, *New American Standard Hebrew-Aramaic and Greek Dictionaries: Updated Edition* (Anaheim: Foundation Publications, Inc., 1998).

[30] Philip Graham Ryken, *Exodus: Saved for God's Glory* (Wheaton, IL: Crossway Books, 2005), 1071.

[31] R. K. Hughes, *Ephesians: The Mystery of the Body of Christ* (Wheaton, IL: Crossway Books, 1990), 166.

[32] John Piper, *Let the Nations Be Glad* (Grand Rapids, MI: Baker Academic, 1993), 41.

Printed in the United States
by Baker & Taylor Publisher Services